Contents

Part 1: Introduction   *page* 5
   The life and works of Tennessee Williams   5
   Background and setting   11
   A note on the text   14

Part 2: Summaries   15
   A general summary   15
   Detailed summaries   15

Part 3: Commentary   29
   The nature of the play   29
   Purpose   31
   Structure   33
   Themes   34
   Characterisation   39
   Style   44
   Context   44

Part 4: Hints for study   46
   Getting to know the play   46
   Approaches to the text and relevant quotations   48
   Preparing and presenting an essay   49
   Specimen questions   51
   Specimen answers   51
   A note on examinations   58

Part 5: Suggestions for further reading   60

The author of these notes   60

Part 1

Introduction

The life and works of Tennessee Williams

'Tennessee' Williams was born Thomas Lanier Williams on 26 March 1911 in Columbus, Mississippi, to Edwina and Cornelius Coffin Williams who both came from the Deep South. His father was of a respectable Tennessee family, hence the son's adopted pen-name. He had served as a volunteer in the Spanish-American War, during which he was commissioned. He worked first with a telephone company, and then as a shoe and clothing salesman on the Mississippi Delta. He married Edwina Dakin in 1907, but she left him soon after to return to the parental home in Columbus where her father, Walter Edwin Dakin, was an Episcopal clergyman. By the time Tennessee Williams was born he had an elder sister, Rose, and his father had begun to drink heavily and to live a loose life in other respects as well, visiting prostitutes and gambling for example. His wife and two children continued to live with the Reverend Dakin, in whose household the young Tennessee Williams heard stories and plays read to him by his mother; had the Bible narratives expounded to him by his grandfather and grandmother; and delighted in the talk of Ozzie, the black maid, about ghosts, evil spirits and 'de debbil'.

In 1918 Cornelius Coffin Williams was appointed to a managerial position in St Louis, Missouri, and he was joined by his wife, pregnant once more, and his two children. Life in St Louis was a great contrast to that in Mississippi. St Louis was an industrial city; they lived in a number of small, dimly lit flats; Cornelius Williams's heavy drinking continued, and he would be foul-mouthed and abusive to his family. Life was very unsettled, and by the time Tennessee was fifteen they had lived in more than sixteen different homes. Edwina Williams was frequently in hospital and suffered from gynaecological problems, while her husband continued to live a riotous life, contracting a sexually transmitted disease on one occasion. This unstable home life caused Tennessee to retreat into an imaginary world of stories and poems, while his sister Rose withdrew into her own mind, which would, eventually, break down entirely. Tennessee began to publish poems and stories in school magazines in 1924.

From 1929 to 1932 he attended the University of Missouri at Columbia, enrolling in the distinguished School of Journalism there in 1931. He discovered the plays of the Norwegian, Henrik Ibsen, and Swedish playwright August Strindberg. Their studies of social ills and their depictions of families in conflict had a profound influence on him. He did not do very well academically, and his father was unwilling to support him beyond 1932, finding him a job with his own company, International Shoe, in the summer. Driving to work with his father he would experience his ill-temper, taciturnity and unwillingness to communicate. Problems of communication between father and son figure prominently in *Cat on a Hot Tin Roof*.

He was intermittently employed at the Shoe Company, spending much time at home between 1932 and 1935, reading and writing. In 1935, during a period of convalescence after a seizure from exhaustion, he discovered the work of the Russian playwright Anton Chekhov with whom he identified closely. He found parallels in the Russian's life with his own unhappy childhood, but also admired Chekhov's ability to reveal a group of characters in emotional crisis, as in *The Cherry Orchard* for example.

In 1935, Tennessee enrolled at Washington University, St Louis, after the family fortunes had improved through his father's promotion. In 1937 Tennessee's first full-length play, *Candles to the Sun*, was performed by an amateur theatre group. A further play which he entered in a competition at the university was not selected for production, leading to his transfer to the State University of Iowa. In that same year his sister was hospitalised after an episode in which her drunk father physically attacked her mother, and made what Rose thought were sexual advances to herself. A lobotomy (an operation to divide nerve tracts in the frontal lobe of the brain) was performed on her, after which she was quiescent, but left emotionally and intellectually a child. The operation had a brief vogue; Rose Williams was one of the first patients to undergo it, but it very quickly went out of use. These sad events obviously had a deep influence on Tennessee Williams, who was very fond of his sister. Many of his plays, among them *Cat on a Hot Tin Roof*, are concerned with family tragedies, violence, sexuality, and a past that troubles the present. Rose's name held a special significance for him, and he uses the rose as a symbol throughout his work, from the title of *The Rose Tattoo*, to the 'rose-silk-shaded' lamp Maggie leaves on when she attempts, at the end of *Cat on a Hot Tin Roof*, to get Brick to make love to her. From 1937 onwards, as Williams's biographer Donald Spoto has said, there could be no possibility of normal life for the family again.

Williams graduated from Iowa in 1938, helping to pay his fees by working as a dishwasher in a local hospital. He lived in New Orleans for a time, enjoying the variety and colour of that city, working at all kinds of jobs, and having his first homosexual experiences. *American Blues*, a collection of short plays submitted to a competition sponsored by the Group Theatre in New York, won a special award while he was living and working in California in 1939. This recognition brought him to the attention of the energetic agent Audrey Wood, who took him on, and looked after his interests for many years. In 1940 he attended play-writing seminars at the New School for Social Research in New York, which also produced *The Long Good-bye*, a short play dealing with the problems of a young writer struggling to overcome a difficult family situation. *Battle of Angels*, a full-length play later revised as *Orpheus Descending*, was produced in Boston in December, 1940–January 1941, its mixed themes of religion and sex outraging some reviewers. In 1941–2 he began to drink heavily, and to spend much time and energy seeking sexual partners on the streets at night, whether in New York, New Orleans, or Massachusetts.

In 1943 Audrey Wood negotiated a six-month contract for him with Metro-Goldwyn-Mayer, the Hollywood film company, as a screen writer, at the then fabulously generous sum of $250 a week. In Los Angeles, between trying to write a movie script for the famous actress Lana Turner he continued with his own work and made friends with Christopher Isherwood. With Donald Windham he wrote *You Touched Me!*, based on a story by D. H. Lawrence, and reflecting his veneration for the novelist whose widow, Frieda, he visited in Taos, New Mexico on a number of occasions. The play was produced in 1943.

He appeared as one of *Five Young American Poets*, published by James Laughlin's innovative New Directions imprint, who remained his publishers. His first major success, *The Glass Menagerie*, went into rehearsals, and opened in Chicago in December 1944, where it nearly closed. However, through the advocacy of friends and the developing performances of the actors the play became a sell-out and moved to New York where it was a hit. *The Glass Menagerie* is an autobiographical play, dealing with a struggling writer who works in a shoe factory, his powerful mother, and his withdrawn sister. Williams himself said that, 'all work is autobiographical if it's serious', and that he was 'more personal' in his writing than most authors. *The Glass Menagerie* of the title refers to a collection of glass animals the sister has in the play, based on a similar collection treasured by his sister Rose.

The New York drama critics circle acclaimed the play as the best of the year. Williams had become famous. In 1946 he became close friends with the novelist Carson McCullers. The following year he met an ex-navy man, Frank Merlo, an association that lasted until Merlo's death in 1963. In that year also *A Streetcar Named Desire*, a title based on the name of an actual tram in New Orleans, opened in New York, to an enthusiastic reception. It was directed by the Hollywood and Broadway director, and organiser of the Actor's Studio in New York, Elia Kazan (*b.* 1909). The young Marlon Brando (*b.* 1924) played the part of Stanley Kowalski, a violent, rude, and energetic man. This play, set in New Orleans, like *Cat on a Hot Tin Roof* reflects Williams's affection for, and obsession with, the values and ways of life of the 'Old South'. Its traditional concerns with courtesy and graciousness are, in Williams's plays, subjected to the harshness, greed, and egoism of a new generation oblivious to those values, or of older people – such as Big Daddy in *Cat on a Hot Tin Roof* – who have deliberately set them aside. In 1948, while in Rome, news came back that *Streetcar* had won the Pulitzer Prize. Around this time he began to use pills to calm himself down or to invigorate him, and he also continued to drink heavily. In the autumn *Summer and Smoke* was produced in New York to a much frostier reception than his two brilliant successes. Frank Merlo and he set up home together in October, and from then on, for many years, Merlo took responsibility for many of the practical details of their life together. Much of 1949 they spent in Italy, where Williams continued to seek out new sexual partners while Merlo was either ill or visiting his family in Sicily: an erotic adventurousness reflected in Williams's first novel, *The Roman Spring of Mrs Stone* (1950), a sombre study of a middle-aged woman's infatuations with a series of young men.

In 1951 *The Rose Tattoo* opened in New York, with Eli Wallach starring. It had wide acclaim. Williams's mother attended the opening night, and was shocked by its explicit sexuality. Her father, the Reverend Dakin, was also present, and he was not at all offended by the play. Curiously enough, the old man was extremely tolerant of his grandson's unconventional private life, often staying for long periods with him and Frank Merlo at a house in Key West, Florida. This somewhat unusual readiness to accept what would be regarded as irregular sexuality by an older man is reflected in Big Daddy's refusal to be shocked at the thought of Brick and Skipper's intense friendship in *Cat on a Hot Tin Roof*.

Later in 1951 in Italy Williams wrote a first draft of a short story, 'Three Players of a Summer Game', about an alcoholic ex-athlete called Brick. This would later become *Cat on a Hot Tin Roof*. The film of *A Streetcar Named Desire* won many awards in 1952. That year he was also made a life member of the National Institute for Arts and Letters, while a revival of *Summer and Smoke* was selling out in New York. However *Camino Real*, staged in 1953, was attacked for its lack of structure, but also because it openly condemned the over-zealous anti-communist campaign being led by Senator Joseph McCarthy.

In early 1954, while staying at Key West, he began work on *Cat on a Hot Tin Roof*, a play which, unlike the somewhat rambling *Camino Real*, observed the formal unities of scene and time. He was now almost totally reliant on barbiturates, alcohol, and stimulants, to enable him to sleep, work, and get on with daily life. In 1955 *Cat on a Hot Tin Roof* was produced in New York by the Playwriter's Company, with Elia Kazan directing, the folk-singer Burl Ives as Big Daddy, and the young Ben Gazzara as Brick. Kazan insisted on some changes to the script (see p. 27 of the 'Summaries' section for an account of the Broadway acting version) which heightened the melodramatic aspects of the play, and helped ensure it was a popular success. The character of Big Daddy – brutal, energetic and vulgar – draws upon Williams's father; while Brick and Maggie contain elements of Williams's own temperament. In the winter of 1955 he worked on the screenplay for the film *Baby Doll* (released 1956), based on previous one-act plays. The film, starring Carroll Baker, Karl Malden and Eli Wallach, and directed by Elia Kazan, created a scandal with its (for the time) explicit sexuality and sado-masochistic overtones, but mostly because of the huge advertising billboard of Carroll Baker in a revealing nightgown. In 1957 his father died. Some years previously this difficult and turbulent man had left Williams's mother, but now Tennessee found himself unprepared for the emotional jolt the bereavement gave him. He began to have psychiatric treatment, and fears of madness increased, his unstable state worsening steadily from drug and alcohol abuse. He visited his sister a great deal at her institution, drawing upon these visits and his psychoanalysis to write *Suddenly Last Summer,* performed in 1958, and filmed the following year by Joseph C. Mankiewicz.

Kazan directed Williams's next play *Sweet Bird of Youth* in 1959, with Paul Newman in the part of Chance Wayne. This met with a mixed reception, estranging some critics by the way in which the characters are used as vehicles for Williams's own opinions, but it ran for a year. By now the tide was beginning to turn against Williams. The taste for romantic questioning and poetic meditation in the theatre was disappearing, to be replaced by an appetite for sharper, more cynical, more intellectual work: the theatre of Harold Pinter in the UK and Edward Albee in America. There was less interest, too, in autobiographical plays, and a greater demand for social realism and psychological analysis.

In 1960 Williams worked on *Period of Adjustment* and *The Night of the Iguana*, the former being produced in that year, the latter in 1961. *The Night of the Iguana* played to great acclaim, and on 9 March 1962 Williams appeared on the cover of *Time* magazine, a major American accolade. Starring Bette Davis and later Shelley Winters, *The Night of the Iguana* was to be his last major success. In 1963 Frank Merlo died of cancer. Williams had become somewhat estranged from him over the past few years, but in the last stages of his illness he spent much time caring for him.

He revised a recent play, *The Milk Train Doesn't Stop Here Anymore*, to turn it into a tribute to his dead friend, but despite the fact that the famous Tallulah Bankhead played the leading role, it closed after a very brief run. Williams re-wrote it for a film version, *Boom*, starring Richard Burton, Noel Coward and Elizabeth Taylor, but this too was a flop. His kind of drama had gone out of fashion, but also the play was a private expression of grief which failed to carry the audience with it. After Merlo's death he retreated more and more into drugs and alcohol. Film versions of his plays had made him wealthy, and the rights for others between 1966 and 1969 earned him 5 million dollars, but for most of the 1960s he went through what he called his 'stoned age'. He was awarded an honorary degree by his Alma Mater, the University of Missouri at Columbia, in 1969. In that year also, possibly partly as a tribute to Frank Merlo, Williams was received into the Roman Catholic Church, though he later denied that he took the conversion very seriously. These years were spent moving restlessly from place to place – New York, Key West, St Louis, Europe, Japan (where he met and was impressed by Yukio Mishima, the novelist who committed hari-kiri, throwing oneself on one's knife, in 1970) – with a variety of partners, but failing to find peace anywhere. Late in 1969 he was hospitalised after a fall while drugged. All narcotics were abruptly withdrawn, and within days he suffered multiple heart attacks and seizures. He recovered, but the experience of being institutionalised deeply unsettled him.

In 1971 he had an argument with Audrey Wood and dismissed her as his agent, accusing her of wanting him dead for ten years. Ever attentive to his best interests, however, she arranged for his affairs to be handled by Bill Barnes who worked in the same agency. A collected edition of his plays in seven volumes began to appear in that year, continuing to 1981.

In 1975 he published the novel *Moise and the World of Reason*, a novel based on Williams's friendships and love affairs, which was attacked for its incoherence. More lucid, if just as self-indulgent, are his *Memoirs*, also published in 1975, in which he frankly describes his sexual preferences and exploits, as well as confessing his addictive and obsessive personality. In the 1970s, a time of expanding sexual liberation, he was venerated in New York and California as an outspoken homosexual, but the politics of gay rights did not appeal to him.

In 1977 he published *Androgyne, Mon Amour*. His play, *Vieux Carré* had a very poor reception that year. Increasingly, he was surrounded by acolytes and disciples, some of whom were devoted to him but many merely attracted by his celebrity or wishing to exploit him. A 1980 play, *Clothes for a Summer Hotel*, explored his relationship with his sister, Rose, although the ostensible characters were the alcoholic novelist Scott Fitzgerald and his wife Zelda. In June of that year his mother died, having suffered years of physical and mental deterioration. He received the Medal of Freedom from President Jimmy Carter in the White House. A 1981 play, *A House Not Meant to Stand*, concerned his father; while *Something Cloudy, Something Clear*, also dealt with lovers and friends, among them Frank Merlo and Tallulah Bankhead. This last play was a success, despite Williams's anxieties that it was too personal.

After receiving an honorary degree from Harvard in 1982 he visited Sicily, intending to travel to the USSR where his plays had always been very popular. He had amassed some £500,000 there in royalties which, because of currency restrictions, had to be spent in Russia. However, he was too ill and exhausted to travel. After a period back in the US, he returned to Sicily in February 1983, wandering around the bars and cafés where he and Frank Merlo used to idle hours away years before. Again, restlessly, he returned to New York, staying at the Elysée Hotel. On 24 February he retired to his bedroom with wine, barbiturates, and cocaine. The following morning he was found dead, a cap from a pill bottle having lodged in this throat and choked him.

Williams was amongst the most successful playwrights in English this century. His work presents a clash between two cultures; the staid secure values of the 'Old South' of the United States, with its manners, courtesy, class system, and privilege, on the one hand; and on the other the modern world of greed, lying, anger, sex, class hatred, and personal spite. His plays depict individuals caught, often tragically, in the collision between these two value systems. But his characters, unlike those of Samuel Beckett or Harold Pinter, are not exhausted by the stresses of these oppositions: they are often forceful or poetic figures, romantic heroes trying to stand up to the difficulties of their situations. Or they are, like Brick Pollitt, enigmatic and sensitive people, who, in their despair retain an ironic edge and a sense of humour. Williams's drama confronts the nastiness of modern life, but it does so without diminishing the value of the individual, and without relinquishing the possibility of love.

His papers are kept at Harvard University.

Background and setting

Cat on a Hot Tin Roof is set in 'the South', an area of the United States which is in many respects a place apart from the rest of the country. It comprises a great block of territory, which taken together forms about one quarter of the US, extending from Missouri in the mid-west to Florida in the south-east; and from Virginia on its north-east edge to Louisiana in the mid-south. The South has its very own proud history, political traditions, economy, folklore, recreation, culture, and dialect. There is a 'Southern drawl', and many agree there is a Southern attitude, which may be characterised as languid, confident, stubborn, proud, even a touch aristocratic. This hauteur can, however, sometimes lift to reveal a passionate and strong-willed force of character, such as we see in Big Daddy, or in Maggie herself, the cat.

The Southern States have a climate which favours the production of crops such as tobacco, cotton, and sugar, all products which, before modern technology made their cultivation less labour-intensive, were heavily dependent upon slave labour. The South resisted the abolition of slavery because its wealth and way of life depended upon it. Large plantation houses (such as the one Big Daddy has earned for himself), big estates, and a mode of life where wealth exercised virtually unquestioned influence, created a society very resistant to the changes that were taking place in the middle of the nineteenth century in America. When Abraham Lincoln, a strong supporter of the abolition of slavery, was elected to the Presidency in 1860, the Southern States began to secede from the Union. Their withdrawal could not be halted and the split soon widened into the American Civil War. Although the Confederate States (the name the South adopted for its alternative alliance to the Union of the United States) was defeated, and the Union re-established, the memory of pride and resistance persisted, giving the Southern character a delight in its independence of spirit, a toughness in adversity, a backward-looking reverence for the past and tradition, as well as a distrust of innovation and modernisation.

We can see these influences at work in Tennessee Williams in two quite opposing ways. First, he inherited a Southern independence of spirit, and despite his unconventional life as a homosexual artist, and his dependence on drugs and alcohol, he was, in many ways, old-fashioned, even stern in outlook. He had courteous and gracious manners; he disliked public displays of immorality and could even be prudish; he liked women to behave like ladies. Nevertheless, alongside this Southern conservatism he also had a Southern independent streak, manifest in his originality, and in his stubborn adherence to a romantic view of human possibility and of love in an American society growing ever more ruthless and avaricious in post-war affluence. He persisted in his own view that drama should attempt to convey emotion and feeling, even though in the 1950s and 1960s the tide of fashion was beginning to flow in the direction of social realism, as in the work of John Osborne in England and Edward Albee in America.

The South took a long time to emerge from the economic setback of defeat in the Civil War. Although blacks were given the vote, there was deep segregation between them and the white community, in spite of the fact that the South as a whole was an economically disadvantaged area, and income per person lagged behind that in every other geographical area of the United States. There were many 'poor whites' as well as impoverished blacks. At around the turn of the century (1900) not only was there extreme poverty amongst the majority of the population in the South, standards in health, education, and housing were also poor.

If we consider the ages of the characters in *Cat on a Hot Tin Roof*, which is set in the mid-1950s, then Big Daddy would have been a very young man at the period of Southern depression. As he tells Brick of his exploits as a bum taking his chances in the railway sidings when a young man, this deprived world of poverty and hardship comes before the audience's mind. We are told how he went to work for the two homosexual plantation owners, Straw and Ochello, how he was taken up by them, made overseer, and eventually inheritor. Big Daddy, then, is depicted as a survivor, someone who has, through effort, determination and charisma, leaped the vast gulf separating the Southern poor (white as well as black) and the wealthy remains of the old Southern plantation elite. That Straw and Ochello are made homosexuals by Williams may be intended to suggest that the old Southern economic drive and strength of character have deteriorated; Williams always retained a residual doubt about the propriety of homosexuality.

And yet, even though Big Daddy seizes his opportunity to take over the estate from Ochello, the heirless survivor of the homosexual liaison, his own energy has not transmitted itself to his sons. Gooper is a functionary and, even though he has children, is a bloodless manipulator rather than a forceful patriarch in the Big Daddy mould. Brick, who seemed to promise something of his father's drive in his sportsmanship and charisma, has become drink-sodden and ineffectual, a man who has given up on life. And, it is made fairly explicit, he has taken to drink because of the unacknowledged homosexuality in his relationship with Skipper, his dead friend, who also became an alcoholic. Big Daddy's appetites for life are large enough for him to accept homosexuality as a feature of some male relationships, but Brick, timorous and defensive at once, cannot tolerate this open-mindedness and opts instead for denial and repression.

The great house itself, surrounded by its massive cotton plantation of 28,000 acres, is a survivor of a past time. Its decline began with Straw and Ochello and their childless liaison. Although re-invigorated by Big Daddy's huge personal energy, the reprieve is only temporary, and the play is concerned with a moment of great crisis for the estate; Big Daddy is to die, while the wives of his two sons bicker over the inheritance; and his two sons are ineffectual in their different ways. These themes of economic and moral decline are part of the emotional background of Williams's play, and help to give it depth and relevance beyond its particular situations. Williams's suggestion that the old secure order, which was established in the nineteenth century, is breaking down, is one widely to be found in twentieth-century literature, from D. H. Lawrence's *Women in Love* (1920) and T. S. Eliot's *Waste Land* (1922) to William Golding's *Lord of the Flies* (1954) and Cormac MacCarthy's *Suttree* (1979). The play vividly conveys a sense of moral, economic, and personal collapse in such a manner as to make it a comment on larger historical phenomena in the modern world. Tennessee Williams, by encapsulating these themes in his characters and their situations, universalises the crisis of a particular family of the Deep South to a portrayal of the modern human condition.

A note on the text

In 1951 Tennessee Williams wrote the first draft of a short story entitled 'Three Players in a Summer Game'. This formed the basis for his play which was to become *Cat on a Hot Tin Roof*, first produced in New York in 1953. Its first publication in Great Britain was in 1956 by Martin Secker & Warburg Ltd, followed a year later by the paperback edition, published by Penguin Books.

The text used for these notes is included in the current Penguin edition of *Cat on a Hot Tin Roof and Other Plays* (published in association with Martin Secker & Warburg Ltd), London, 1976.

Part 2

Summaries
of CAT ON A HOT TIN ROOF

A general summary

Big Daddy, owner of the extensive Pollitt plantation in the Deep South of the US, has been ill for some years. Brick, his younger son, married to Maggie, is an alcoholic, while Gooper, the elder boy, is married to Mae, and they have five children. Big Daddy has not made a will and Gooper and Mae plot to secure his estate for themselves, even though Brick has always been the favourite son. News comes that Big Daddy is not suffering from cancer, as was feared, which appears to crown the celebration of Big Daddy's birthday. Maggie, the 'cat on a hot tin roof', is desperate to get part of the estate for Brick and herself. She tries to break through Brick's alcoholic stupor by revealing that she and Skipper, Brick's dead friend, were lovers, and by announcing that she wants a child of her own.

We know that Big Daddy's cancer is real, but he, released as he thinks from the jaws of death, plans to enjoy himself. He and Brick engage in a long discussion during which Big Daddy tries to probe the reason for Brick's alcoholism. He dismisses Brick's own explanation, that he is disgusted with the lies people tell each other and themselves, and points to a harsher truth, that Brick has not faced the sexual nature of his friendship with Skipper. Shocked at his father's forthrightness, Brick tells him the truth about his illness – that he has cancer and will die.

Now Gooper and Mae attempt to assemble a family conference to implement a draft plan for the trusteeship of the estate which they have drawn up. Big Mama refuses to allow this, in spite of her distressed state in finding that her husband has cancer after all. To everyone's surprise Maggie announces that she is pregnant. Overjoyed, Big Mama goes to tell her husband, who roars out in agony as the pain descends upon him. Maggie gets rid of all Brick's liquor and tells him he can drink again when he turns her lie into truth.

Detailed summaries

Act One

All the action takes place in the bedsitting room of a plantation mansion in the Mississippi Delta, which is owned by Big Daddy Pollitt. The estate is the biggest in the Southern states of the US, extending to 28,000 acres of the best land, the 'richest land this side of the valley Nile', as Big Daddy says in Act Two. Unusually for a modern play there is one setting throughout, the bedsitting room, and the action is continuous across the three Acts. No lapse of time occurs between the Acts and each of them is itself continuous, that is, there are no scene divisions. This unity of scene and time helps sustain the pace of the action and contributes to its feeling of hectic intensity.

As the play opens Brick Pollitt, Big Daddy's younger son, is taking a shower in the off-stage bathroom, while Margaret his wife (known as Maggie in the play) complains about her brother-in-law, the comically named Gooper (suggesting someone lumbering, foolish and dull) and his pushy wife Mae. One of the Gooper children – whom Maggie refers to as 'no-neck monsters' – has messed up her dress, while all five of them were made to show off for Big Daddy, whose birthday they are celebrating. Brick comes on-stage as Maggie is forcefully explaining to her alcoholic husband that Gooper and his scheming wife are trying to push him out of his inheritance. Big Daddy has been ill for some years, and cancer is suspected, so, Maggie explains, Gooper and Mae have seized the opportunity to outflank Brick.

They take every chance, she says, to damage his reputation, referring constantly to Rainbow Hill, a refuge and treatment centre for alcoholics. Brick, we learn, as Williams packs information into Maggie's outraged account of Gooper's greedy tactics, was once a sportsman, an American football professional, then a sports announcer on television, but now he has stopped work to concentrate on drinking. His behaviour is detached and irresponsible: he is indifferent to the manoeuvres of Gooper and his wife, and in a drunken spree the night before he has broken his ankle trying to jump hurdles on the athletic field. Throughout the play we are reminded that Brick is a wounded man, both physically and psychologically. Maggie, however, is far from beaten – she will not turn a blind eye on the game Gooper and Mae are playing, and is intent on fighting her corner. She also suspects that Big Daddy shares her disgust at the 'no-neck monsters', and at the cloying insincerity of Mae's only too obviously displayed maternal feelings. Additionally, Maggie has a suspicion that Big Daddy finds her sexually attractive, a suggestion that adds a further complicated twist to a set of family relations that already is being revealed as explosive and dangerously volatile. 'Way he drops his eyes down my body when I'm talkin' to him,' she says '. . . an' licks his old chops! Ha ha!' Brick finds this kind of talk disgusting, an indication that he is uncomfortable with sex and that he has something to hide, which will emerge soon enough.

Maggie goes on to tell Brick, who has now stretched himself out on the bed, all that went on at the supper, during which Gooper's children were being put through their paces. She describes and acts out how Brick's brother and sister-in-law exchanged 'signs an' signals' so openly that even Big Mama, not 'the quickest an' brightest thing in the world' in Maggie's phrase, notices that something odd is going on. Maggie then goes on to tell Brick (and the audience) that Mae does not come from a very respectable family in Memphis: all they ever had was money, and her father lost that, narrowly escaping imprisonment for shady dealing on the stock market. In the middle of her mocking and energetic outburst she catches him looking at her in a way that, she says, 'froze my blood'. Williams doesn't explain this look that Brick gives her (students might ask themselves what Brick is meant to convey in that gaze) but he denies that it has any significance. She then goes on to say that she has changed, that she has gone through 'this – hideous – transformation', she has become cruel and hard in order to cope with her husband's drinking and his remoteness from her. She is, she says, 'lonely'. Now the conversation, entirely led by her, moves into very dangerous territory: Brick's friendship with Skipper. It starts off innocently enough, with Maggie saying that, unusually for a hard drinker, Brick has not become fat, although both admit that eventually drink will soften him up. Earlier in the play, Williams tells us in a stage-direction, that 'His liquor hasn't started tearing him down outside', implying that the destruction is well underway inside. She mentions that Skipper had begun to deteriorate physically, but then stops short, and instead describes the attitude and demeanour Brick has developed in drink: a 'detached quality', a 'charm of the defeated'. What precisely has defeated him is left hanging in the air, for the time being, but by now the audience is intrigued by the scrap of information she has blurted out, that it has something to do with his friend Skipper. She, however, protests that she is not defeated, that she is 'determined to win'. She describes herself as a 'cat on a hot tin roof', whose victory, she says, is in 'just staying on it for as long as she can'. She returns to the look Brick gave her, and forces the issue, asking if he was thinking of Skipper when he looked at her the way he did. Brick does not answer, taking a drink instead, while she declares that the 'laws of silence don't work', implying that he cannot drown whatever is destroying him in alcohol. He merely pours himself another shot, as he waits for the 'click I get in my head' when he has enough to make him peaceful. (The reader should refer to the introduction for an account of Williams's own heavy dependence on alcohol.)

Mae now rushes in, carrying Maggie's bow, which she won at a University archery contest when she attended 'Ole Miss' – Mississippi University. It's called the Diana Trophy and identifies her with the Roman goddess of archery, hunting, and, strangely, childbirth, seeing as so far she is childless. The athletic associations of Diana, as a deity who loved to run on foot with her hounds, is deliberately linked to Maggie, who says that 'I love to run with dogs through chilly woods'. This classical reference underlines her energy and determination, as well as hinting that she is, despite his defeat, a suitable mate for an ex-athlete.

She recommences her attempts to try to persuade Brick to join Big Daddy's birthday party, only to drive him to comment that she is becoming tiresome and spoiling his liquor. He urges her to take a lover, but she wants more than mere fulfilment of sex and desire. They have agreed to live together (or rather 'occupy the same cage' as she says) on condition that he and she do not live as husband and wife, a condition to which she cannot reconcile herself. Maggie locks the door to face him down on the issue, but just as she is pushing the moment to a climax Big Mama knocks. Big Mama is overwhelmed by news from the Ochsner Clinic, that Big Daddy does not have cancer after all, but that he has a spastic colon (see glossary), a relatively minor condition compared with what was feared. Big Mama, telling Maggie how grateful she was when she heard the news, shows her her bruised knees, having dropped her huge weight on to them in thankful prayer. Brick has taken the precaution of going into the bathroom as soon as his mother enters where he remains until her conversation with Maggie is over. Big Mama announces that they will now hold Big Daddy's party in the bedsitting room because Brick cannot get downstairs with his broken ankle. Fussily, the old lady starts to tidy up; then she checks with Maggie by gestures if Brick has been drinking, concerned that he may overhear. However she goes on to say that Brick never drank until he got married. To this, Maggie responds with a shout, *'THAT'S NOT FAIR!'*; but then Big Mama asks if she makes her son happy in bed, asserting that all marriages that go on the rocks do so because of sexual dissatisfaction. Big Mama sweeps out; Maggie, appalled, steadies herself by looking at herself in the mirror, saying to herself that she is 'Maggie the Cat'.

The coast now clear, Brick comes out of the bathroom and immediately refills his glass, whistling as he does so. He remains detached as Maggie continues to look at herself in the mirror, appraising her own good looks, and telling him she has had offers from other men. Once more he makes it clear to her that she is free to leave, but she reminds him that he has no money to face divorce expenses, save what he gets from his father, who, she says, to the audience and Brick's surprise, is dying of cancer after all. The message from the clinic is a false one, to fool Big Daddy and to help him fool himself that he is not dying. She reveals that the real situation, which Gooper and Mae are also aware of, will be made known to Big Mama tonight. Brick's brother and sister-in-law hope to oust Brick from the inheritance and the circumstances are made all the more complicated by the fact that Big Daddy has neglected to make a will.

Maggie now confesses that, in spite of his coarseness and bad language, she has always admired Big Daddy. We learn from her that he moved into the plantation as overseer for the previous owners, Jack Straw and Peter

Ochello, homosexuals who lived in the bedsitting room she and Brick occupy now, and in which the action is set. Ghosts haunt the scene. Big Daddy has remained in essence what he was: a tough and hard businessman, and nobody's fool, a 'red neck' (see glossary). She, like Big Daddy, is facing the facts, knowing that 'it takes money to take care of a drinker', and that the only chance of getting it is Big Daddy. She is all the more resolute in this determination because she has been '*so God damn disgustingly poor*' all her life. She knows about the expense of drink, because her father wasted their family's wealth indulging his weakness. It is possible to be indifferent to money when young, but to be old and poor is, she says, 'just too awful'.

This realisation of how desperate her situation is leads dramatically into the climax of Act One, when she admits to Brick that she made a mistake in telling him about what happened between herself and Skipper. Up to now he has never allowed her to speak freely about his friend – it is a 'dangerous thing to do' – but now she does so.

She and Skipper, she says, were both in love with Brick, and so they went to bed together to be closer to him. Pressing on, insisting that the story has got to be told, she describes the friendship between the two young men as 'beautiful, ideal things they tell you about in the Greek legends', but what made it sad was the fact that it could never be carried through to anything satisfying or even talked about plainly. In spite of the protestations that she respects homosexual love, Brick accuses her of 'naming it dirty'. She continues however, by saying that she understands how pure their love was, so pure that it killed Skipper, death being the 'only icebox where you could keep it'. She relates how Skipper and she went to a game in Chicago, Brick being incapacitated by spinal injury; and how she confronted Skipper with the fact that he loved Brick. He slapped her, but later went to her room where he had sex with her, in an attempt to prove that what she had said about him was not true. But from then on he was destroyed, unable to face the truth about himself, and turned to drink and drugs.

Dixie, one of Gooper's children, bursts into the room wearing an Indian headdress and shouting. When Maggie tries to restrain her the child exclaims, thereby revealing the intimate conversations of the Gooper household, that Maggie is jealous because she 'can't have babies'. The Cat now turns to Brick just before the curtain, to say that she has been checked by a gynaecologist, and that now is a perfect time to conceive. She is not only a huntress, out to get what she can for her man; she is also a goddess of fertility who wants a child: she is Diana.

NOTES AND GLOSSARY:
deliquescence: fading (good looks)
Great Smokies: mountains in Tennessee: a National Park

ev'ry whipstitch:	everything
power-of-attorney:	power to control all his finances
AP or UP:	press agencies
contrapuntal leisure:	contrasting ease
twilight sleep:	a state induced by an injection, which obliterates any sensation of pain, but without loss of consciousness
'lech':	short for lechery, sexual urge
his old chops:	lips
fleecing a sucker:	swindle someone stupid
Spanish news:	American colloquialism meaning bad news
pen:	penitentiary, prison
banshee:	Irish spirit, said to haunt certain families. She appears when a member of the family is close to death, and howls
my hat is still in the ring:	I'm still ready to contest
Diana:	Roman goddess of hunting, and as a derivative, of running. She also symbolises chastity, mating and childbirth
Ole Miss campus:	Mississippi University
***spahkluhs*:**	Southern American phonetic rendition of sparklers, a small firework carried in the hand
Shoot:	go on
spastic colon:	a condition of the intestines where the gut contracts uncontrollably, causing discomfort and pain to the sufferer
highball:	an iced drink of whisky and soda water
red neck:	American colloquialism of the southern states meaning a rough person from the country, often violent, always white
Echo Spring:	type of liquor
Job's turkey:	in the Old Testament of the Bible Job loses all his riches; so Job's turkey would be very poor indeed
***Vogue*:**	international fashion magazine
***sashays*:**	flounces

Act Two

The action flows directly on after the break, with Big Daddy, Gooper, the Reverend Tooker, Mae, 'Doc' Baugh the family doctor, Big Mama and the children all assembling in the bedsitting room for Big Daddy's birthday party. Maggie vainly tries to create a party atmosphere by putting some music on the Hi-Fi (see glossary) only for Big Daddy to assert his dominance over the whole household by roaring at her to 'turn that damn thing off!' Big Mama also tries to establish a party atmosphere by pulling the Reverend Tooker – who is preoccupied with getting church donations for stained glass and central heating – onto her fat lap, but Big Daddy orders her to stop this horseplay. In a stage direction Williams tells us that in spite of the relief of having the all clear from the clinic he still has the '*same old fox teeth in his guts*', an allusion to the belief, held in some quarters, that cancer is parasitic. Champagne and a cake are brought in, Gooper's children sing for Big Daddy, and Big Mama starts crying from happiness at the good news they have had. Maggie breaks the embarrassment by presenting her father-in-law with the dressing-gown she claims is a present from Brick, although Mae reveals that Maggie herself has bought it to save her husband's face.

Big Daddy is, however, much more preoccupied in finding out if what he has heard is true, that Brick has broken his ankle while jumping hurdles on the athletic field in the middle of the night. Crudely, he asks if he was having sex with someone on the cinder track, ignoring Big Mama's concerns that he will upset the Reverend Tooker. Maggie now tries to bring things round to normal again by asking the old man to blow out the candles on the cake, only to provoke another outburst of rage. Big Mama's remonstrations and protests are met with a further onslaught of fury, as Big Daddy accuses her of trying to take over during his illness when they all thought he was dying.

There now follows a scene of emotional revelation, punctuated by a firework display, organised for Big Daddy's birthday. He warns Big Mama – and this gives Williams an opportunity to sketch in details of Big Daddy's early life in a tirade of embittered hatred from the old man – that he will not easily give up what has been so hard won. He recalls working like a 'nigger' in the field, having left school at ten, how he acted as overseer with Straw and Ochello, and how he then became Ochello's partner when his friend died, and expanded the plantation. Big Mama protests that she has truly loved him, even his hardness and hate, all through the years, but now she realises that he never believed she did. When she exits, weeping, Big Daddy wonders if what she has said is true.

The tension is broken by renewed explosions of fireworks. Big Daddy is now alone on stage; everyone else is watching the display. He calls for Brick and Maggie brings him in from the balcony, giving her husband a kiss before she leaves again. Brick wipes it off. Now Big Daddy and his younger son begin the conversation that is to dominate the remainder of this Act.

Big Daddy opens by remarking that Brick and Gooper have each married the same type of woman, to which Brick responds by saying that Maggie and Mae are both like cats on a hot tin roof, facing each other, each determined to get most of Big Daddy's estate for their respective men. Mae is eavesdropping at the balcony door, and Big Daddy confronts her with the fact that she and Gooper, who have the room next to Brick's, spy on him and Maggie, reporting back to Big Mama on what they hear, who in turn passes it on to the old man. Big Daddy knows, from this source, that Brick and Maggie do not sleep together. In response to Big Daddy's probings Brick admits he has a drink problem, while his father warns him that a man who drinks too much is throwing his life away when there is nothing else to hold on to except life itself. A clock strikes ten, which sets Big Daddy off on a series of recollections of a trip he and Big Mama took to Europe, when she bought the clock and much else. Europe was, he says like a big auction, a huge fire-sale, where anything could be got, provided there was money enough to pay for it. In Barcelona there were children begging, while in Morocco (actually in North Africa, not Europe, though Big Daddy lumps it together with Spain) an old Arab woman offered him her tiny child as a prostitute. The old man is talkative because, he says, he has had a new lease of life; Brick then describes what he likes to hear most of all: 'solid quiet'. We learn that Brick and his father have had these exchanges before but that they have proved inconclusive in the past. 'Communication', says Brick, is 'awful hard between people', which could be a summary of one of the main themes of the play (see 'Themes' in the 'Commentary' section, p. 34). As if in corroboration of Brick's point Big Daddy admits that he thought he was dying but kept a 'tight mouth about it'. When Brick asks what advantage there is in that, Big Daddy cannot reply, save to say that a 'pig squeals', but a man can, sometimes, hold his peace about his suffering. And yet, ironically, man is the only creature who knows what death is.

Resolving now to enjoy what life is left to him, Big Daddy takes a whisky highball (see glossary for Act One) and looks forward to taking his pleasure, particularly in sex. Big Mama tries to come back in but he holds the door against her. When she leaves, sobbing, he imagines what it will be like with a young woman, whom he will 'smother in minks', and 'choke with diamonds'. When Brick announces that he is still waiting for the 'click' in his head, which indicates he has enough alcohol to make him peaceful, Big Daddy realises that his son is 'alcoholic', a word that Brick easily accepts. Big Daddy vows to sort this out, now that he knows he is not going to die. Brick wants to be free of this conversation which, he says, is going round in circles, but Big Daddy insists he explains why he drinks, taking Brick's crutch from him so he cannot easily move. Eventually the son declares that he drinks out of 'disgust with mendacity', that is, disgust with lying and liars. At first Big Daddy thinks he is referring to some specific lie or lies he has been told, but when Brick reveals that he is speaking generally about widespread deceit his father shows little patience with his sensitivity. The old man declares that most of life is composed of mendacity: he has had to pretend that he loved Big Mama, that he likes going to church, that he enjoys clubs such as the Elks and Rotary. These observances, he maintains, are all 'crap'. He has lived with mendacity so why cannot Brick. There is nothing else to live with except lying. To which Brick responds that there is something else: drink. In this exchange Big Daddy admits that despite the mendacity of his life he always has had some respect and affection for Brick. They both acknowledge that they have never lied to each other, despite Brick's reservation, but also that they have never really communicated.

Williams then moves the psychological focus a few notches up in intensity, to render more clearly both Brick's problem and the growing understanding between the two men. Brick admits, in response to Big Daddy's relentless questioning, that when he was younger he could live with the world's deceit because he believed. When pressed about what he believed in Brick cannot answer, at which point his father releases the bombshell: that Brick started drinking when Skipper died. Williams now tells us in a stage direction that Brick's remoteness and detachment are broken through, and goes on, somewhat ponderously, to announce that he is seeking to '*catch the true quality of experience in a group of people, that cloudy, flickering, evanescent – fiercely charged! – interplay of live human beings in the thundercloud of a common crisis*'. Despite the slightly overwritten language, this is a good summary of the entire play.

Big Daddy suggests that Brick and Skipper were homosexuals, but goes on to say that he can understand such things, recalling his early life as a travelling hand, living and sleeping rough. This outrages Brick even more, and he accuses his father of calling him a 'queer' (see glossary). Incongruously, this moment of heightened tension is deflated by the Reverend Tooker coming in and asking for the gentlemen's lavatory. When he goes, Big Daddy returns to the story of his early life, to Jack Straw and Peter Ochello, and how when Straw died his friend stopped eating. He wants Brick to know that he can understand love between men but this only drives Brick into even greater fury, such that he falls over. Big Daddy extends his hand to help him up in a symbolic gesture of fatherly understanding.

Brick is appalled that his father can be so casual about a thing which he feels is monstrous. He insists that Skipper and he had a true friendship and that that was what was abnormal about it, rather than any sexual deviance. He admits that they shared rooms, that they sometimes touched but he is emphatic it went no further. Then, if that is so Big Daddy asks, why did both Brick and Skipper crack up? They are now, Brick says, going to have the true facts Big Daddy wanted. Maggie, he says, resented the friendship between them, and on the day Brick was injured, she put into Skipper's mind the suggestion that they were homosexual. To prove this was not so, Brick says, Skipper slept with her, and when this failed Skipper became convinced she was right and drank himself to death. Big Daddy knows Brick is holding something back, who now admits there was a drunken telephone call in which Skipper confessed his love. Brick hung up.

Big Daddy announces that they have now tracked to its source Brick's disgust at mendacity: it is a disgust with himself. In revenge the son now blurts out that Big Daddy is dying and that he has cancer after all. He tries to take it back, but it is no use. The act ends with Big Daddy screaming in rage at all lying sons of bitches. A child is struck and it runs across the stage, bawling, as the curtain falls, symbolising the child that each of the two men has hurt in the other.

NOTES AND GLOSSARY:

Tiffany: glass by Louis Tiffany, American artist (*d.* 1933)

Hi-Fi: short for high fidelity, a term used to describe advanced sound reproduction, particularly of music, in the post-war era; a record player

the Delta: the region of the Mississippi Delta

the Stork and the Reaper: the stork is used to symbolise birth, the Reaper death

humping: having sexual intercourse

cuttin' you'self a piece o'poon-tang: Southern US slang for having sex

nigger: Southern US (derogatory) colloquialism for black, now generally avoided

big fire sale: giant auction after fire damage

blue chip stocks: stocks that sell at a high price because of public confidence in their long record of steady earnings

jag: slang term for a bout, often drinking, but here talk

shootin' th' breeze: Southern US slang term for talking in a rambling fashion

gas: American slang term for talk

the old man made out of bones: death symbolised as a skeleton

bull: short for bullshit – nonsense

ball: American slang term for a good time

Skid Row: a squalid urban area which is a meeting place for down-and-outs

balled up: American slang for being in a mess

Elks! Masons! Rotary!: Elks: American businessman's club, akin to Rotary; Freemasons: a world-wide secret society of men who pledge to aid each other in business; Rotary: an international association of businessmen, founded in the US in 1905 to promote civil and community service

jig: dance

passing the buck: evading the issue

evanescent: fading

hobo: American slang for vagrant or tramp, often taking rides on freight trains

railroad Y's:	cheap boarding houses near railway stations in the US (from YMCA, Young Men's Christian Association hostels)
flophouses:	cheap boarding houses
queer:	derogatory slang term for male homosexual
gin:	a machine that separates the seeds and hulls from the cotton fibres
sodomy:	anal sexual intercourse
ducking sissies:	male homosexuals
Fairies:	as above
shako:	a tall headdress
bursitis:	inflammation of the joints
lush:	drunkard

Act Three

As with the previous act, Act Three continues with no lapse of time. Mae and Big Mama come in from the fireworks display looking for Big Daddy. Big Mama makes excuses for his behaviour, saying that he is worn out from strain. Gooper, Maggie, Doc Baugh, and the Reverend Tooker also enter, and there is a discussion of Brick's drinking, Big Mama saying that he has never recovered from Skipper's death. She is taken aback when she realises that Brick has overheard the comment. He pours himself yet another drink, still waiting for the 'click'.

Gooper gets Doc Baugh to tell the family the truth about Big Daddy's condition, that he has an incurable malignant cancer. Big Mama will not accept that her husband is going to die, so that when Gooper attempts to begin discussion of a plan he has drawn up for the management of the plantation she refuses to listen. Gooper and Mae vilify Brick as immature and irresponsible and unfit to take over the running of the estate, while he is out on the balcony, still drinking. Not to be diverted from his purpose, Gooper states his case as the elder and more reliable son, acknowledging that he was never Big Daddy's favourite in the way that Brick was. He wants, he says, a fair deal. Meanwhile Brick comes back in, to the sarcastic and malicious comments of Mae and Gooper.

Pleading pressure of time – he has to return to Memphis the following day to resume his duties as corporation lawyer – Gooper outlines the legal arrangements he has drawn up (a trusteeship of the estate) whereby, as Maggie bitterly points out, he will be in charge of everything and dole out funds as he sees fit. Big Mama, however, will have none of this, and orders him to put away his proposed plan, calling it, in the word Big Daddy uses to express his disgust, 'crap'. No one will take over anything until Big Daddy dies, she says, and maybe not even then.

Brick is singing softly to himself 'Show Me the Way to Go Home', a song associated with drunkenness, as Big Mama gazes on him, remarking that he looks now just as he did when a little boy, after playing 'wild games'. She is struck by a realisation of how fleeting time is, and remarks that they should all love each other and be as close as possible. She embraces Brick, while behind her stands her other son, Gooper, 'tense with envy'. Heedless of the effect she is having on Gooper, she implores Brick to give Big Daddy a grandson, saying that it would be his 'fondest dream come true'. Furiously, Mae zips up the briefcase containing the trusteeship plan, caustically remarking that Brick and Maggie cannot oblige.

However, Maggie now takes centre stage to announce that she and Brick are to have a child after all. Overcome with this news Big Mama rushes out to tell her husband. Maggie fixes Brick another drink while Gooper and Mae accuse her of lying to fool a dying man. A roar of agony and rage from Big Daddy signals that the terminal pain has struck. Mae and Gooper go out to see to him, leaving Brick and Maggie alone.

She thanks him for not contradicting her announcement, while he, after gulping down three shots of whisky in quick succession, announces that the 'click' has finally arrived. Maggie now takes command while Brick is out on the balcony, singing to himself, and empties the liquor cabinet. When he comes back she announces that his addiction has made her stronger than he. She gives notice that she wants to conceive, informing him that she has consulted medical opinion, and that this is the best time of the month for her. She tells him that drink will be withheld until she has what she wants from him. Big Mama rushes in, to snatch up the morphine Doc Baugh has left behind to dull Big Daddy's pain, and to kiss Brick, whom she now thinks is a father-to-be.

When she exits Maggie declares they will make the lie come true, and when they have done so, they will get drunk together. She declares her love for him, Brick remarking, echoing an earlier line of Big Daddy's: 'Wouldn't it be funny if that was true?'

NOTES AND GLOSSARY:

cawn-bread: corn-bread made from cornflour in the Southern US

molasses: a thick brown syrup derived from sugar-cane during refining

hoppin' john: a dish consisting of meat such as bacon, ham or pork-knuckles, and peas cooked together and seasoned with red pepper. First recorded in 1838

yams: a tropical or sub-tropical plant, the tubers of which are eaten. These are sometimes referred to as sweet potatoes and may be either boiled or roasted

Keeley cure: treatment for alcoholics, named after a Dr Keeley

'Annie Bust' tablets: a drug therapy for alcoholism which stops the break-up of toxins normally occurring in the body so that the patient experiences the fully poisonous effects of alcohol. The treatment was pioneered by Eric Jacobsen in Denmark

sodium amytal: a chemical compound used as a sedative

morphine: an opium extract used as a painkiller

hypo: hypodermic syringe

uraemia: accumulation of waste products in the body, that are normally passed in urine

shenanigans: treacherous or mischievous doings

Sugar Bowl: a misnaming of Rose Bowl (see below), revealing Gooper's total lack of interest in sport

Rose Bowl: American sports stadium

trusteeship: being a trustee, someone who holds a legal right to act on someone else's behalf

scat song: jazz singing using improvised meaningless syllables instead of words

---

Act Three (Broadway Version)

When the play was staged on Broadway in New York in 1955, it was directed by the famous producer, Elia Kazan, a friend of Williams. When Kazan saw the first draft he had reservations about Act Three and asked the playwright to rewrite the script with this in mind. Kazan's doubts about Act Three were as follows: he felt that Big Daddy should not disappear after Act Two; that the impact on the exchange between Big Daddy and Brick in Act Two should have an effect on Brick's character in Act Three; and that Maggie should be made a more clearly sympathetic character. Williams did rewrite to incorporate Kazan's suggestions.

In the Broadway acting version of Act Three Big Daddy does reappear. He tells a bawdy story about an elephant's state of sexual arousal as an ironic commentary on the childless Maggie and Brick, which provokes Maggie into making the false claim that she is pregnant directly to Big Daddy himself. He responds by asking Gooper to bring a lawyer on the next working day so he can make his will, leaving all to Brick now that he is to have a child. When Gooper and Mae challenge Maggie about the truth of her declaration, Brick joins in his wife's deception. Brick, in this rewritten version, is therefore much less passive than in the other, indicating the degree of William's compliance with Kazan's view that the shattering scene between Brick and his father in Act Two should have worked some deep-rooted change.

Altogether the Broadway Act Three is much more eventful – there is a violent storm taking place for a good part of it; Brick says he wants to take treatment for alcoholism in Rainbow Hill; and Maggie throws the whisky bottles off the balcony. On the whole, the original version is more powerful and more credible. Bringing Big Daddy on in Act Three is less effective than the howl of agony off-stage as the pain strikes. Also, Brick's despair is so deep that it is hard to believe that a conversation, no matter how shattering, could have such an immediate effect. Finally, the writing in the first version is strong enough not to need the somewhat obvious theatricality of a storm.

Part 3

Commentary

The nature of the play

It is difficult to pin down the exact nature of *Cat on a Hot Tin Roof*. As a piece of dramatic writing it has elements of tragedy and comedy. Williams himself probably thought of it as being mostly in the tragic mode, because he deliberately chose to observe the classical unities of time and place (or scene), marked features of Greek and Roman tragedy. The time the play takes to act corresponds with the events as they unfold. There are no flashbacks, no narrators telling the audience information it needs to make sense of the action. All the events take place in one place, the bedsitting room occupied by Brick and Maggie. There are no changes of scene, no lighting effects to enable the audience to imagine other places or circumstances. Setting and action sequence are very tightly focused in order to maximise the audience's concentration on the lives of the characters as they are being revealed on stage.

Are these lives tragic? Tragedy may be defined as a dramatic form in which the main character (or characters) is made to confront crucial aspects of reality which they have hitherto failed to take into account. For that reason their lives, up to the point of realisation, have been lived according to a false premise, an illusion, a lie they tell themselves or which is told to them by others. The moment when the realisation dawns, when the hero (or heroes) has to face the actuality of his or her situation is called, by Aristotle in his *Poetics*, a moment of 'discovery'. It involves a complete and most often drastic reassessment of their life. In tragedy this discovery is either made too late for anything to be done about it, or people are so set in their ways that they cannot summon up the will or resolve to adapt to the new information provided. In comedy some resolution is found. Either the characters can change, or an outside force compels them to. Oedipus, in Sophocles's ancient Greek play, written in about 450BC, finds out too late that he is married to his mother for anything to be done about his situation, other than suffer and eventually die; in Shakespeare's *The Winter's Tale* (1610) Leontes is sorry for his jealousy and his wife is returned to him when he thought he had killed her, a comic resolution to a potentially tragic action.

In *Cat on a Hot Tin Roof* a number of characters 'discover' (in Aristotle's sense) something crucial about themselves, which they have not faced before. Brick discovers, is brought face-to-face with, the nature of his relationship with his dead friend, Skipper. Does he change on account of it? This was precisely the matter that caused Elia Kazan anxiety when he looked at Williams's draft typescript for the Broadway production (see 'Summaries', p. 27). Kazan felt that such a stupendous 'discovery' in Act Two should lead to a different Brick in Act Three, a more active, more energetic, more decided character. Williams obliged to some extent, giving Brick more resolve in a rewritten Act Three for Broadway. In other words Kazan wanted a happier ending, a more 'comic' outcome. But Williams could not transform the character he created, who is essentially tragic, in that he cannot cope with the discovery presented to him in Act Two because he cannot change very much. Williams's own instincts as a writer were correct when he stuck to the first version for the published text, because Brick is a tragic hero, someone blind to a crucial aspect of his life, who cannot (like Hamlet) galvanise the will to act even when his father, his wife, and his own best interests are demanding that he break out of his drunken 'detachment'.

The play is also Big Daddy's tragedy. He is presented with two discoveries: a false one followed by a true one. At first he gets the report from the clinic that he does not have cancer, that he actually suffers from a spastic colon, but subsequently, Brick, in retaliation for the unwelcome discovery Big Daddy has forced upon him, tells his father the truth about his illness. This revelation drives Big Daddy into a thunderous rage: there is not the slightest possibility that such a man, tempestuous, greedy, lustful, and full of appetite, will accept this new reality. In Act Three, off-stage, he howls against his pain.

There are comic elements in the play to lighten its often grim intensity. There is the incongruity of Big Mama's horseplay with the Reverend Tooker: she, an amply endowed, hefty woman, acts like a sixteen-year-old flighty schoolgirl with the solemn and single-mindedly greedy clergyman, even shortening the title 'Preacher' to the embarrassingly inappropriate 'Preach'. Or there is the crude and black humour of Big Daddy's total disregard for Big Mama's feelings. Maggie, too, has resources of comedy: she mimics the scene of the birthday table for Brick when Gooper and Mae tried to impress Big Daddy with the talents and charm of their children, called by Maggie the 'no-neck monsters'. Her insistence that Brick take some action towards the close of the play indicates that she is not a tragically passive character, in the way he is. More like Big Daddy in his health, she is energetic, resolved, steady, not tragic.

This play, then, is a drama which is predominantly tragic in its outlook but which is lightened by comic elements. It observes the classical unities of place and time, and has a major tragic hero in Big Daddy. Brick may, ultimately, be a tragic figure too but this depends on whether he and Maggie can draw strength from their individual suffering and unite to produce a child, thus securing their future.

Purpose

Tennessee Williams has stated quite explicitly the purpose that underpins all his writing in a preface, entitled 'Person-to-Person', which he wrote for a selection of his plays. Recalling a group of little girls dressed up in their mother's clothes he once saw on a sidewalk in Mississippi, he remembers how one of them, not satisfied that she was getting enough attention from her companions, screamed out 'Look at me! Look at me!' and then fell over unable to balance on the outsize high heels. That, for Williams, sums up what southern American, and indeed all, writers do. They want people to be interested enough in what they have to say to look at them and listen to them. This urge to communicate is not only Williams's underlying purpose in all he wrote, including *Cat on a Hot Tin Roof*: it is also his dominating theme (see section on 'Themes', p. 34). Brick and Big Daddy at first fail and then succeed, tragically, in communicating in this play.

Williams goes on in 'Person-to-Person' as follows:

> I want you to observe what I do for your possible pleasure and to give you knowledge of things that I feel I may know better than you, because my world is different from yours, as different as every man's world is from the world of others . . .

Williams wants his audience to look at and listen to his particular set of communications, because his view of things is different from all other views of the world, and he is intent at getting across his particular vision. He wants to do this not necessarily out of vanity (which might appear to be the case at first sight) but because his angle on life is different from other angles, just as each individual person has an individual and unique perception. Drama is an especially suitable form for presenting the individual world-view of each person. Characters in plays are preoccupied with telling others what life is like for them. They try to get others to believe what they believe, or to convince themselves that they have done so successfully.

Dramatic conflict arises when two different perceptions of the world are brought together: Shakespeare's King Lear thinks his daughters love him, it is the story he tells himself; only to find that his interpretation of the situation is radically different from what is the case. Brick in Williams's play has one view of his past, but his father has quite another, and Williams opens up the gulf between these two attitudes and lets human misery pour out of it into the action on stage. To take another set of perceptions, Brick has one view of his marriage – something routine, sterile, to be endured – but this is being continually challenged by his wife, Maggie, who wants something more, in particular a child. Or there are the comically different views of Gooper and Mae of their family respon-sibilities to those of Brick and Maggie. Gooper is all striving greed, action, deceit; while Brick, indifferent, lazy, and forthright, is given focus by

Maggie, who, unlike Mae, actually likes her father-in-law. Every character in the play has a different outlook and the drama is an organic and shifting mechanism whereby all points of view are played off against each other (notice the appropriateness of the word 'play'), so that we can see a complicated human situation from all angles, 'in the round'. The theatre, better than any other form, presents us physically with the differences between people, and between what people think to be the case and what actually exists. A play is a field of differing viewpoints, and *Cat on a Hot Tin Roof* is a good example of such a field.

The kind of communication Williams seeks to accomplish in his drama is not, at its best, merely a personal confession – although his lesser plays failed because they tended to be over-emotional and too tangled up with his own concerns. His finest work presents the members of the audience with a living enactment of their own problems in communicating with others, in a manner to which they feel drawn in a personal, intimate way and with which they can identify. In 'Person-to-Person' he writes that he has a:

> ... highly personal even intimate relationship with people who go to see plays ... I don't want to talk to people only about the surface aspects of their lives, the sort of things that acquaintances laugh and chatter about on ordinary social occasions.

He wants drama to move beyond the 'discretion of social conversation' into an arena where individual views of the world emerge, and collide. That collision is dramatic excitement and tension. Each of the three acts of *Cat on a Hot Tin Roof* has one such major collision and a number of minor ones (see 'Structure' in this section).

In the 'Notes for the Designer' for *Cat on a Hot Tin Roof* he says that the set should be primarily a background for a play dealing with 'human extremities of emotion', which puts the whole play into a nutshell. In a long stage direction in Act Two, just before Big Daddy and Brick begin to face the gap that exists in their perceptions of each other and themselves, the great set-piece of this act, leading up to the explosive, all-out, confrontation, Williams is quite explicit about what he is after in this play:

> I'm trying to catch the true quality of experience in a group of people, that cloudy, flickering, evanescent – fiercely charged! – interplay of live human beings in the thundercloud of a common crisis.

Kazan in the Broadway production picked up the hint about thunder, and to increase the level of intensity Williams wrote in a storm as background for Act Three. However, the 'thundercloud' in this play is not necessarily a literal one: it is the lowering cloud of human feelings before they burst into extremity.

Structure

The play is a three-act tragic drama which observes the classical unities of time (the action is continuous and stage-time reflects real-time) and scene (the action is carried forward in one place). For details of these larger formal concerns, which relate to the definition of the type of play this is, see 'The nature of the play' in this section.

Tennessee Williams has made it clear that his purpose (see previous section) is to engage the audience's attention to make them focus on 'the true quality of experience in a group of people' in a way that will impress the audience deeply. His structure serves that function. Structure, in a work of art, is the dynamic interrelation of all the parts to achieve an artistic end. An artist or a playwright arranges his materials on the canvas or on the stage for maximum impact.

In *Cat on a Hot Tin Roof* the three-act structure is used to reveal different aspects of the complicated human situation, each act concentrating on giving the audience insights into specific groupings of characters and the interactions or collisions between them. Act One concentrates upon the 'quality of experience' in the marriages, with the focus primarily on that between Brick and Maggie, contrasted with the Gooper–Mae marriage, and the Big Daddy–Big Mama one. However, we only know of the latter through Big Mama until Act Two, as Big Daddy is not brought on until that act. This is another good structural device because the audience hears a great deal about him before it sees him in all his grossness and vulgarity. In Act Two Big Daddy shows disparagement for his wife. The Brick–Maggie marriage is shown to be deeply unstable, and the reasons for that instability are revealed as the act progresses, which reaches a climax in Maggie's admission that she has committed adultery with Brick's dead friend Skipper, who, she says, was in love with Brick. The act concludes in violence, with Brick trying to hit his wife. Gooper and Mae would appear, on the surface, to have a most worthwhile marriage. They have five children (shortly to become six) and he is successful in business. However they are driven by greed and envy. Big Mama is overjoyed when she learns (falsely) that her husband does not have cancer, but we also hear of a Big Daddy different from his wife's sentimentalised view of him from Maggie, who describes him as a strong, if silly, old man who is still lecherous.

These three different marriages provide the basic human materials of the play. The other acts deepen our understanding of them, concentrating on various interrelations between these partners and others. Act Two shows the Big Daddy–Big Mama marriage to be based on a tragic illusion on her part, and little more than convenience on his. His impatience with her emerges, but the main structural focus in this act is the relationship between father and son, Big Daddy and Brick. We have seen in Act One and in the opening of Act Two that the Big Daddy–Big Mama,

Brick–Maggie marriages are unstable, and the major dramatic interest of Act Two centres on the reasons for this instability. The long exchange, dominating the action, between Brick and his father, reveals two deeply injured men: one – Brick – unable to cope with his relationship with his dead friend; the other – Big Daddy – unable to communicate with his son. Neither of them can cope with their lives, and this inability leads to the rage which they turn upon each other in the open conflict between them that concludes the act in shouting and fury.

In the Broadway Act Three these 'extremities of emotion' were underlined by the somewhat melodramatic device of a storm accompanying the action as the play races to its close. In the published text the emphasis lies starkly on the contrast between the marriages of Gooper and Brick, and Big Mama's adjudications between them. Gooper has his proposal for the trusteeship, which is rejected by Big Mama; Maggie has her device for survival, her lie about being pregnant, which Big Mama embraces. Her favouring the 'prodigal son' Brick is underlined in a structural stage-arrangement just before Maggie makes her mendacious announcement: Big Mama embraces Brick, while Gooper stands behind her holding his briefcase, as she is oblivious of his presence. Once again this particular piece of structural staging, as well as the entire structural emphasis of the act on the plottings of the two married couples in order to survive, emphasises the ways in which Williams has thrown the spotlight on the lack of communication between individuals in particular human situations. Structure, in other words, serves purpose and theme.

Interestingly, each act ends with a child, the shrieking daughter who insults Maggie in Act One; the child who is struck in Act Two; and Maggie's phantom baby at the end. By contrast to the other two acts, Act Three ends in a mood of curious and forlorn hope, as Brick and Maggie prepare to turn her lie into a reality.

Themes

Communication and Lies

Lack of communication between people is a major theme of the play. Brick and Maggie have a marriage based upon non-communication. He has retreated into the hazy half-world of alcoholism; he is 'detached', remote, observing the 'laws of silence'. Despite the fact that their marriage, in his mind, is based on both of them observing these 'laws' she is determined not to accept this situation of mutual non-communication. All he waits for is the 'click in the head' when the alcohol works, and he becomes quiet in his silence. She resents this 'charm of the defeated' which he cultivates. Her hat, she says, 'is still in the ring'; she is determined not to fail, but 'to win'. This determination is the keynote of her character (see 'Characterisation', p. 39).

Communication between people, in this play, is often based upon lies. This is the reason Brick gives for his alcoholism in Act Two, when pressed by his father. He is, he says, disgusted with 'mendacity'; it is the basis, in his view, for, he says hesitantly, 'the whole thing', meaning that all of society is based on false communication or lies. Big Daddy is deeply impatient with this, because as far as he is concerned that observation is so self-evident as to be trite. He has had continually to live according to lies: pretending to love Big Mama, Gooper, Mae, and their children – the 'five screechers out there like parrots in a jungle'. Big Daddy is experienced in mendacity, claiming there is 'nothing *else* to *live* with'. However, he maintains that there is real communication between Brick and himself; that they, at least, have not lied to each other, and therefore pushes Brick towards the admission that he is deceiving himself about the reason for his drinking. He presses him to admit, in the structural climax of Act Two, which focuses on the nature of communication itself, that the reason Brick has given himself for his drinking is a distraction from the truth. The truth is that he failed to face the fact that Skipper was homosexual and loved him. Brick's reaction to this emotional bombshell is extreme (in line with Williams's comment that the play deals with extremities of emotion). He points out that Big Daddy, for all his experience of mendacity, has himself been duped into believing that he does not have cancer, when the truth is that he is dying. Act Two, therefore, comes to a climax at a point when the gap in communication between father and son is made searingly evident.

It's all the more ironic that this should occur between these two characters. 'Communication', says Brick, 'is – awful hard ... between you and me, it just don't – ', and he stops there, his sentence trailing off, not able to find the words. We learn that, despite the difficulty, they have in the past continually tried to make contact. However, because Brick observes 'laws of silence' and Big Daddy's code is to keep 'a tight mouth' ('a pig squeals, but a man ... can keep a tight mouth'), they have tended to go around in circles. The exception is this occasion when each reveals a tragic 'discovery' (see 'The nature of the play, p. 29).

Most of characters in the play fail to communicate with others effectively. Big Daddy's entire family is based on lies or non-communication. The parents themselves have little common understanding; indeed Big Daddy tells Brick that he has pretended to be in love with his wife, even at the most intimate moments. He accuses her, when the (false) news comes that he has the all-clear from the cancer clinic, of wanting to take over the house and the estate. For three years, he says, she has been 'Sashaying [her] fat old body around the place [he] made'. His colon has been made spastic, he claims, by disgust at all the lies he has had to put up with from her, pretending to love him, when all she wanted was to get him out of the way. She is appalled at this:

BIG MAMA: *In all these years you never believed that I loved you??*
BIG DADDY: Huh?
BIG MAMA: *And I did, I did so much, I did love you!* – I even loved your hate and your hardness, Big Daddy!
BIG DADDY [*to himself*]: *Wouldn't it be funny if that was true . . .*

Williams leaves the matter there; the yawning gulf between them all too evident. He marks it dramatically with an explosion of one of the fireworks being set off for Big Daddy's birthday. The complete lack of any ground of communication is emphasised further in the exploratory conversation between Big Daddy and Brick, when the old man declares that he is going to enjoy sex to the full with some young mistress he will 'smother in minks' now that he believes he is not going to die.

Gooper and Mae are intent on getting what they can out of the situation that has arisen: Gooper's father dying, Brick's alcoholism, Big Mama being confused and upset. They are not at all concerned with trying to respond to or communicate with anyone other than making their children perform to impress their grandparents. They have a simple message they want to get across: that Gooper is the best person for trusteeship of the estate so he can control the money and cut Brick and Maggie out of any significant settlement. Doc Baugh is a liar, and the Reverend Tooker is out for what he can get in order to improve his church facilities. It is hard not to agree with Big Daddy at the end of Act Two that, apart from Brick and Maggie, they are 'ALL – LYING SONS OF – LYING BITCHES!'. When Big Mama does, tearfully, embrace Brick in Act Three saying 'you know we just got to love each other an' stay together', she does so with her back turned to Gooper who is, Williams writes in a stage direction, '*tense with sibling envy*'.

The Past

It is a quality of a good dramatist that the past lives of characters are sketched in vividly, whether through dialogue, reminiscence, or characterisation, so that the audience can appreciate fully the personal and emotional circumstances that influence behaviour as the action proceeds. The dramatist wants to present as rounded a picture as possible of the people he creates on stage, and that involves careful and telling evocation of their past lives. Here Williams achieves this not by change of scene or flashback but by powerful reminiscence.

In *Cat on a Hot Tin Roof* many characters have troublesome pasts, dark secrets, hidden histories of which they themselves are sometimes unconscious. But the house itself and the estate have a history. Big Daddy tells

us, when he accuses Big Mama in Act Two of trying to take over control
of the estate, that he will not easily give up ownership of something he has
fought so hard to win. He tells us, forcefully and briefly, how he left school
at ten, then went to work for the owners, Jack Straw and Peter Ochello,
rising to overseer. We learn later in the act that these two men were
homosexuals, and when Brick is outraged that his father should think that
he and Skipper were homosexually involved, he accuses Big Daddy of
putting Maggie and him in their old bedroom, because he thought Brick
was 'queer' like them. Their sexuality does hang over the marriage of
Brick and Maggie. Skipper did love Brick, and confessed to it; Maggie
loves him, and at the end of Act One suggests that she and Skipper became
lovers because they both loved Brick. This complicated sexual tangle is
shadowed by the love between the two dead men.

It is also suggested that Big Daddy had at least some familiarity with
homosexual love. When he suggests there may have been 'something not
right' in Brick's friendship with Skipper, Brick is enraged and defensive.
Williams has a long stage direction at this point, to the effect that a central
nerve in the emotional complex of the play is touched, and that Skipper
may have had to die to allow Brick to 'keep face' in the world. To defuse
the tension Big Daddy tries to suggest that he would not be too upset by
such elements in his son's personality, because he, a man of the world, has
had much experience of the strangeness of human nature. The implication
is that he did not disapprove of or was in no way put out by the two men
who 'took (him) in', going on to say, before he is interrupted, that he can
'understand such – . . .' Brick, however, continues to be outraged, and to
challenge his father that what is being inferred is that he and his friend
were 'queers', 'fairies', who '. . . did – *sodomy*!'

Maggie is closely involved in the secret of Brick's past, but she has a
sexual history of her own as well. She tells Brick in Act One that Big
Daddy himself would appear to have sexual feelings towards her. When
she goes on to confront Brick with the fact that she and Skipper were
lovers because they both loved him, he protests that she is vilifying something 'good' and 'true', friendship.

Loneliness

The theme of loneliness is most relevant to the significance of *Cat on a
Hot Tin Roof*. Central to the play's meaning is the problem that lies at the
heart of the dialogue between father and son in Act Two: the difficulty
of people communicating with each other. If people cannot communicate then they are condemned to solitude and to silence. When the play
opens we are confronted with a man who has sunk into the privacy and
self-containment of addiction, compelling his wife to observe the 'laws
of silence'. Nothing must disturb his solitude; he wants to remain in

isolation. Maggie tries to awaken Brick out of this alienation not only because she is lonely, being deprived of any real communication with him, but also because she realises she needs to restore him to some kind of relationship with humanity if she is to secure their future together. It takes money to take care of a drunk, as she knows from the bitter experience of her own childhood when her father was also an alcoholic. If she cannot bring Brick into some normal relationship with human society he will lose the estate to his acquisitive brother Gooper and his wife, Mae.

As is evident in the competitiveness displayed in Gooper's grasping attitude; in Maggie's dismissive stance towards her brother-in-law's children; and in Mae's sneakiness in letting Big Daddy know that Brick's marriage is in serious trouble, this is a family in which most of the individuals are just that, individuals, with no familial sense or fellow feeling. Big Daddy reveals how much he hated Big Mama; while the Reverend Tooker, even, hangs around waiting for a handout for his church. Each person is locked into an isolated world of private absorption or self-interest; so that there is hardly any communication except through confrontation, and loneliness is the dominating condition.

There are a number of points when it would seem as if contact is about to be made but all of these are submerged in a storm of rage and denial with the possible exception of the last instance. The first instance of the possibility of contact to break the isolation of loneliness occurs in Act One, when Maggie confronts Brick about his friendship with Skipper. She tries to shock him into human realisation by getting him to face the fact that Skipper loved him, as she did and still does, but he reacts by trying to hit her.

The second instance occurs in Act Two during the long dialogue between father and son. The father, showing more 'tolerance' than his son towards homosexuality and human experience in general, tries to make contact with Brick, and seeks to explore the reasons for his drinking. Like Maggie in Act One he presses his case until he gets Brick to admit that there was a drunken telephone call in which Skipper, his old college-friend, confessed to loving him. But this admission is immediately followed by Brick's brutal retaliation in telling his father that the all-clear from the clinic is false, and that he is dying. Big Daddy reacts by proclaiming all to be liars, while human contact, the abatement of loneliness that has been achieved, is blown away.

The last occasion when the isolation that surrounds these frantic characters is breached occurs right at the end of the play, achieving a mood of fragile hope. Maggie tells Brick that now that he's an alcoholic she is stronger than he is, a strength which allows her to love him 'more truly'. She takes command, removing his liquor and promising to return it only when he has attempted to make real what she has asserted was the case: she wants him to make her pregnant, thereby securing the estate. Brick, wonderingly, complies, amazed at her force and determination, and ready, at the fall of the curtain, to entertain the possibility of love. This is the one shared moment of true empathy in the play and the fact that it occurs at final curtain makes it ambiguous as well as resonant and powerful. Will Brick leave his loneliness and come into humanity? The question is left open.

Characterisation

Characterisation, and the interactions between characters, is the means whereby the dramatist explores the human experience that lies at the heart of theatre. The different worlds, as Williams put it in 'Person-to-Person', that characters carry around with them collide and interact, and if the dramatist succeeds 'the true quality of experience in a group of people' (as he describes it in his long stage direction in Act Two) will become evident. It will become clear that characterisation is closely linked to the way in which a writer develops his 'themes' to achieve his 'purpose' within the 'structure' of human interest and plot. Where appropriate, cross-references to these sections are given in discussion of each character.

Brick

Brick is an alcoholic who has retired to a 'remote', 'detached' and drink-sodden world. He lives according to a 'law of silence' (see 'Communication and Lies', p. 34), much to the fury of his wife, Maggie. So great is the gulf that separates him from the rest of humanity that he lives a separate emotional life from his wife. He is caught in the grip of the past (see 'The Past', p. 36), the nature of which he finds very difficult to face. His wife is deeply anxious that his indifference, the 'charm of the defeated' that he possesses, will allow his brother Gooper and his wife, Mae, to relieve him of any part in the settlement that will follow his father's death from cancer.

Her attempt to arouse him from this remote lethargy is the main substance of Act One, and consists in her confronting him with a view of his relationship with his dead friend Skipper that causes him great distress. She says that his friendship with Skipper was 'one of those beautiful, ideal things they tell about in the Greek legends', but that in actual fact both she and Skipper loved Brick sexually, and that that was why they became lovers.

Refusing to face this revelation, Brick is made to confront another 'discovery' (see section on 'The nature of the play', p. 29), in Act Two, the set-piece of which is the exchange between Big Daddy and Brick. There Big Daddy seeks to probe the reason for Brick's alcoholism, dismissing his answer that he is drinking to escape from his disgust with lies, lying, 'mendacity'. Eventually Big Daddy forces him to face the fact that he has been 'passing the buck'. He drinks, his father says, because he failed to face his friend's homosexuality with him, omitting to tell Big Daddy of the detail of a drunken phone call from Skipper, when his friend confessed his feelings for Brick. Big Daddy puts it bluntly: 'This disgust with mendacity is disgust with yourself.' Brick retaliates, in a rage, by telling his father that he is going to die of cancer after all.

Throughout the play Brick is waiting for the click in his head, which signals he has enough alcohol to make him peaceful. Quite often he disappears off-stage, onto the balcony, when a situation develops that he wishes to avoid. In Act Three, as Gooper and Mae try to implement the plan that will cut him out of the estate, he is off-stage, drinking. At the end of the play the click arrives at long last, at which point Maggie decides to make the lie that she is pregnant a reality, irrespective of Brick's wishes or inclinations. As Maggie describes him at the close, he is weak and beautiful, a passive character who, in spite of the fierce shock administered by Big Daddy in Act Two, remains essentially passive, remote, and detached.

Maggie

Maggie is the 'cat on the hot tin roof' of the title, and she is such because she is restless, anxious, and worried. Her husband lives a 'remote' and detached life, sunk in alcoholic oblivion, while she is only too aware that unless he pulls himself together his opportunistic brother Gooper and his ruthless wife Mae, will cut him out from his father's estate. When Brick tells her to jump off the hot tin roof, he thinks that she is impatient for another man, that she is restless because she is unsatisfied, but that is not so. She 'can't see a man but you', she says, and refuses to reconcile herself with the conditions he has imposed for their life together: sexlessness and detachment.

She is 'determined to win', and will not accept defeat in the way Brick is ready to do. She is still a consciously attractive woman, who admires herself in the mirror and knows other men do too, even, she thinks, Big Daddy. She tries to jolt Brick out of his refusal to face the fact that Skipper loved him by telling him of her affair with his dead friend, and gives notice that she wants him to make her pregnant with the child that will ensure a place in the inheritance for them both. At the end of the play she seizes the initiative by locking away all Brick's liquor, promising only to let him have it once more when he has performed his sexual duties. She is energetic, witty, warm, and comic. She acts out the ridiculous birthday scene of the 'no-neck monsters' for Brick, and recalls her own poverty. Because she knows what it is to be poor she is determined that she and Brick will not lose out on what should be theirs, in part at least. She understands money, saying to Brick: 'You can be young without

money but you can't be old without it . . . to be old without it is just too
awful.'

She is aware that the emotional sterility of life with Brick has made her
hard. She calls this a 'hideous transformation'. She is 'catty', she says,
because she is 'consumed with envy and eaten up with longing' – envy for
those, like Gooper and Mae, who have children and who (as happens at the
end of Act One) have no compunction about rubbing salt into the wound;
and longing for children of her own and for warmth and kindness in her
marriage. This combination of feelings and ambitions makes her like the
goddess Diana, with whom she is briefly associated in the play. Maggie is
fierce, determined, beautiful, without children, a free spirit; and yet, also,
she is longing for children; similarly, Diana is the goddess of fertility as
well as the hunt.

Big Daddy

Big Daddy is one of Williams's monumental creations. Big in size,
personality, desire, appetite (we are told how much he eats at his birthday
party), he also owns the huge Pollitt plantation: 'Twenty-eight thousand
acres of the richest land this side of the valley Nile', a phrase used a
number of times to describe the extent and opulence of his estate. He is a
patriarch, like an Old Testament Egyptian king, not afraid to indulge
his whims, lusts, and tempers. These Old Testament associations are
strengthened by the reference to the Nile, the ancient river of Egypt. He is
impulsive, irascible, venal; but he is also curiously broad-minded and
unshockable.

He does not appear on stage until Act Two during which he and his
favoured son, Brick, engage in the attempt at communication which
occupies the main focus of dramatic interest. We hear of him continually
in Act One so that when he does appear in Act Two the structural impact is
all the greater, as the set-piece on the theme of communication takes place.
He and Brick are two tragic characters in the play (see 'The nature of the
play, p. 29), and it is through their interaction that Williams's central
dramatic purpose (see 'Purpose', p. 31), is achieved: catching the 'true
quality of experience' between people.

Like a patriarch he regards women as of little account. He rudely
rebukes his wife for flirting with the Reverend Tooker: '*WILL YOU QUIT
HORSIN'?*' he roars, going on, 'You're too old an' too fat fo' that sort of
crazy kid stuff . . .' His reaction to the birthday cake the black servants
bring in and to Big Mama's tears of joy at the celebration is brutally funny:
'Now Ida, what the hell is the matter with you?' Instead of beaming
joyfully at the fuss being made of him he wants to know how Brick broke
his ankle, and openly asks him if he was misbehaving with a girl on the
cindertrack the night before. When Big Mama tries to bring back some

decorum and festivity to the occasion, Big Daddy tells her to quit this, saying he will behave and talk just as he wishes. He has a renewed energy now that he thinks the curse of cancer has been lifted, and when he is alone with Brick, confesses his determination to indulge in Old Testament patriarchal lusts to the full.

Like Isaac in the Bible, who favoured Jacob over Esau, Big Daddy prefers Brick to Gooper. Thinking he was dying of cancer, he has not, by his own admission, been paying sufficient attention to his son, and is even unaware of his alcoholism. In Act Two, therefore, he presses him into a conversation during which the two men confront the lies they have been telling themselves, or by which they have allowed themselves to be duped. Brick is made to face his probable homosexuality, Big Daddy the fact that he is dying after all. (For further discussion of this crucial conversation see the sections on 'Structure', 'Themes', and 'Brick' above.)

In Act Three (published version) Big Daddy does not appear but we do hear him howling, off-stage, as the terminal pain hits him. In spite of his statement in Act Two that a man can keep a 'quiet mouth', here it is made dramatically evident that there are occasions of human suffering when that may not be possible.

Big Mama

Like Big Daddy, Big Mama is a larger-than-life figure. She is physically big ('fat' according to Big Daddy), loving, affectionate, sentimental, and loyal. She is shocked when her husband (whom she now believes cured of cancer) in Act Two accuses her of wanting him out of the way so she can take over the estate. She protests her love for him, even saying she loved his 'hardness'. In Act Three Gooper and Mae arrange it so that Doc Baugh tells her the truth of her husband's condition. Her reaction is explosive. She rejects Mae and Gooper, turning to Brick, whom she names her 'only son'.

Her affections, like those for Big Daddy, are focused on him, because, Williams tells us in a stage direction, both men make themselves loved by the 'simple expedient' of not loving enough to disturb their 'detachment'. This statement is slightly confusing, and also indicates that Williams is worried that his dramatic action may not be making it clear why Big Mama finds herself devoted to men who are self-absorbed and not a little cruel. Does Williams succeed in showing us how a woman like Big Mama can love two men so unresponsive as Brick and his father? Students will wish to ponder this question, but it may be that Williams's own experience is involved in this somewhat less than satisfactory characterisation. His own mother Edwina (see 'Introduction', p. 5) gave much of her life to the service of a charming but drunken and brutal man, and this is surely reflected in the sympathetic but somewhat baffled treatment of Big Mama, just as Big Daddy owes something to Cornelius Coffin Williams. Williams himself always admitted that his work was deeply autobiographical and personal. Big Mama shows impressive fortitude and control in resisting the attempt Gooper and Mae make to take over the estate.

Gooper

Gooper is Big Daddy's eldest son, and the Esau to Brick's Jacob (see the discussion of Big Daddy as patriarch, above). He is a lawyer in Memphis, staying at the family home, during the final stages of his father's terminal illness. He and his wife, Mae, are intent on acquiring for themselves the 'trusteeship' of the estate, on the not unreasonable grounds that Brick is an alcoholic and Big Mama something of a hysteric. Gooper is a solid family man, with five children by Mae and another on the way. This respectability is undercut however when we learn, from Big Daddy, that Gooper and Mae have been eavesdropping on Brick and Maggie, then going along to Big Mama and telling all the details of their unhappy marriage, knowing that she will pass them on to her husband.

Gooper is envious of Brick's place in his parents' affections. He plans his strategy carefully to achieve his ends using a lawyer's skill to weaken his prey. He gets Doc Baugh to tell Big Mama the truth about Big Daddy's illness, then, calculating that she will be vulnerable at this point, produces a 'plan' from his briefcase, only to have it soundly rejected by his mother. Not only is the plan rejected, but he is too, when she calls Brick her 'only son', cutting Gooper out of the embrace in Act Two. She holds Brick, while behind her stands Gooper, seething with jealousy.

Mae

Mae is Gooper's wife and collaborator in the plan to gain the trusteeship of the estate. She rehearses her children (Maggie's 'no-neck monsters') to perform for Big Daddy's birthday party, hoping to ingratiate her family with him, only to have the opposite effect. She is, for Maggie, a 'monster of fertility'. Maggie also lets us know that Mae Flynn (as she was) comes from a none-too-respectable background. Her father, whose only claim to status was money, lost his wealth and narrowly avoided prison for 'shady' dealing. She, like Maggie, knows the value of money, and will stop at nothing to get it.

Reverend Tooker and Doc Baugh

The Reverend Tooker is out for what he can get, and Doc Baugh is the instrument of the strategic lie Gooper and Mae use, unsuccessfully, to demoralise Big Mama.

Style

Williams uses the speech of the 'Old South', the southern states of the US, to give colour to the language. The 'Old South' has a tradition of emphatic and rhetorical speaking, a tendency to declamation, insult, and vigour which Williams uses to dramatic effect in *Cat on a Hot Tin Roof*. Maggie speaks openly and bluntly, saying for example, that Big Daddy 'licks his old chops' when he looks at her. Big Daddy tells his wife to stop 'horsin' around', and he is not afraid to bellow out his rage and hatred. Brick has the languid air and easy drawl of an Old Southern grandee, soused in liquor. The main characters in the play are vital, dynamic, their speech is full of energetically expressed feelings and prejudices, all of which create a mood and style appropriate to the depiction of a powerful family in a state of crisis.

Context

The play was first produced in 1955, and it reflects many of the concerns, attitudes, and changes in post-war American society. The play depicts a family in crisis, divided against itself. The family, as an institution, was coming under increasing attack in the years after the Second World War. With affluence growing in western society, and particularly in America, a culture was developing which placed emphasis on the individual as opposed to society and the family. Where younger people before the war, in the 1930s, were expected to suppress their own desires for the good of the family and society, in the 1950s an appreciation was developing of the value of self-expression and individualism. In America this individualism, associated with jazz, became known as 'cool'. There was the 'cool' jazz of Miles Davis and Gerry Mulligan, and it was 'cool' to be self-absorbed, detached, remote, and indifferent to society's needs or family values. Maggie, infuriated by Brick's alcoholic detachment says to him: 'You look so cool, so cool, so enviably cool.' He has the 'charm of the defeated', the kind of relaxed air of cool indifference that had begun to become fashionable in Paris, New York, and London. Existentialist philosophers, such as Jean-Paul Sartre, became popular arbiters of manners, and their emphasis on disillusionment with western capitalism and social structures appealed to young people eager to shake off the restraints of convention, family life, and morality. Brick, calmly accepting what life has done to him, on the surface at least, is a product of 1950s' youthful detachment.

Brick's cynical detachment from concerns over money and status, has, we know, a deeper reason, other than fashionable indifference. He is disillusioned with a system based, he says, on lies, but the reason underlying these protestations is his unhappiness about the nature of his friendship with Skipper. The 1950s was a time when homosexuality, although still to some degree a taboo subject, was beginning to be more generally acceptable in the atmosphere of increasing sexual and personal freedom that followed the Second World War. Although Brick in the play finds it hard to face his own probable homosexuality, the fact that Williams can write what became a hugely successful play on the subject reveals a change in social and moral values.

The corruption evident in the Pollitt family with Brick alcoholic, Big Daddy lustful and brutal, Gooper amoral and grasping, Maggie determined, and Mae calculating, presents a picture of American life in crisis. There was a sense in the 1950s that the power vested in the institutions of state and family could destroy humanity, and the Pollitt family imploding offers a comment on a society which, with the invention of the atomic bomb, could destroy itself.

Part 4

Hints for study

Getting to know the play

Getting to know a novel or a poem is so much a matter of reading and re-reading that people often assume that you can treat a play like a novel or poem. But the text of a play is not the play itself, since most plays, and certainly *Cat on a Hot Tin Roof* falls within this category, are designed to be seen in performance. Plays designed for reading rather than for acting have been written by poets and novelists, but Williams was not primarily a poet or a novelist (although he was also these things) but a man of the theatre, which, as the Greek origin of the word reveals, is a place where people go to see things happen before their eyes. The theatre is a place where actors recreate moments of rare insight, bafflement, tragedy, comedy, exhilaration, and despair: the entire range of human feelings and thoughts. Why humans invented the theatre, and why we like going there to see people acting things out when we know that what they are pretending is not actually happening at all, are questions well worth thinking about carefully. Also worth pondering is the question as to why a writer chooses drama or theatre as a medium rather than poetry or the novel. It will surely have something to do with the physicality of theatre, the fact that on-stage live people are *embodying* the thoughts and feelings generated by crisis or difficulty (and usually plays are concerned with confronting a difficulty) rather than ruminating on them or describing them. Showing something by physical action and speech is much more compelling than describing it in writing, no matter how vivid the description.

Only in a performance will the student be able to see the dramatic contrast between Big Daddy's bulk and powerful energy and Brick's hesitant guilt, as he works his way around the stage with the aid of his crutch. Also, that other crutch of Brick's drink becomes much more real to us when we see him compulsively heading to the liquor cabinet whenever he is questioned too closely, or when an awkward question demands to be answered.

The contrasts between the three main women of the play will also become more pronounced: Maggie's iron determination and her will, which make her not unlike Big Daddy in temperament; Mae's scheming deliberation, and her attempts to use her children as visible testimonials to her's and Gooper's claim on the land because they have a family; and Big

Mama's soft desperation, suggested by her huge soft body, itself a contrast to Big Daddy's combination of fat and forcefulness.

It would be possible for students to perform this play for themselves, or with the help of a kind (and patient) lecturer or teacher. Students studying this play are unlikely to be as experienced in life, or as old or as generously endowed physically as Big Daddy, so casting him, even for a walk-through reading, will not be easy. However, fun can be had with his role (and that of Big Mama's) by students attempting to assume his patriarchal airs and blunt force and her emotionality and ludicrous playfulness. Also Brick's role, of aimless drunk, will provide opportunities for enjoyment as well as reflection; and the two young women, Maggie and Mae, offer vigorous and interesting parts.

Though some study, concentrated revision for instance, is a solitary activity, most is not, and indeed study of the drama is often best when it is most sociable. Very few students need to study alone; it should be possible for most readers of the play to get together with others in order to stage, in however elementary a fashion, their own performance. Even simple reading round the class will serve to clarify matters greatly, but it is better to try to achieve a 'proper' performance, in which actors move about within a designated play-area. Such a performance need not be at all elaborate. More elaborate still would be a performance with a stage-set and costumes. The construction and making of these will also serve to increase knowledge of the play because it will encourage students to think about dramatic effects. Why for instance does Williams finish Act Two with a child running on stage, then off, with the fire-crackers, shouting? He wants to shock the audience, but is there more to it than that? Also, dealing with the practicalities of props and costume will make use of the talents of those students, often among the best, who find acting a burden.

Above all, throughout the process of putting on the play, actors, extras, and stage-hands should be encouraged to talk about what they are doing. If they are encouraged then interesting questions, of far-reaching significance, will often be raised in the most casual manner. Perhaps you have more actresses than actors in your class and want to give some of the men's parts over to women; but should you allow Brick to be played by a girl? What problems would this raise? Whether or not a polished performance is the result of all these deliberations is of no great moment: what matters is the increased likelihood of everyone's seeing the play not as marks upon a page but as spoken words, as movements across a stage, as first one grouping of actors and then as another. What may well have seemed merely dull in the reading will suddenly take on life: what had seemed insignificant will be found to have point and purpose; stage directions, which in a printed version are a part of the text itself, will disappear in order to carry out their silent task of marshalling the action.

A few students, because of the time at which they are obliged to study or because of the remoteness of their homes, may be unable to join with others in this sort of activity. Even they, however, must not rest content with a simple reading of the play. At the very least they should read it aloud, seriously attending to variations in emphasis and intonation as they do so (Williams's stage directions are useful in this respect). A better idea is to construct a simple model theatre (it need be nothing more difficult to obtain than a table-top) within which figures can be moved about. Such a model, though a poor substitute for seeing the play in performance, will allow it to be experienced as a series of happenings in space as well as in time, for it is the spatial aspect of theatre which a mere reading of a text, however patient that reading may be, cannot suggest adequately. If a model theatre and toy actors smacks uncomfortably of playing with dolls, you might comfort yourself by trying to consider how well this image of dolls that are played with by forces which they are powerless to resist sums up what is happening in Williams's play, which deals with the powerful impact on people's lives of moral and economic decline, illness and death.

Approaches to the text and relevant quotations

Students should remember the overriding purpose that Tennessee Williams declared as his objective, right at the dramatic heart of the play, the moment when the exchange between Big Daddy and Brick is at its most intense. In the stage direction which precedes this emotional extremity, a structural high-point in the play, Williams says that he wants to capture the *'true quality of experience in a group of people'*. Everything in the play, structure, purpose, themes, characters, revolves around that central objective. Williams as a dramatist wants to be a kind of surgeon, cutting away the diseased parts of human nature to get at what he considers to be the core realities, and they, in his view, have to do with the experience of people as they interact. A poet may concern himself with the nature of individual perception, a novelist with men and women in society, but playwrights deal primarily with the actualities and dynamics of human relationships.

Human relationships in *Cat on a Hot Tin Roof* are in a critical condition; marriages are unstable (see 'Structure', p. 33, above); communication is difficult, Brick saying, 'Communication is – awful hard between people . . .' Society seems built upon lies, Big Daddy declaring to Brick 'there's nothing else to live with except mendacity'. When the family congratulate Big Daddy on his birthday his monosyllabic response is 'crap', a word he uses frequently to express his disgust at falsity and pretence. Maggie, 'the cat', would agree with Big Daddy. For her, morality is based on people pretending to be good, and it is only the rich who can afford moral positions: 'The rich or the well-to-do can afford to respect moral patterns . . . but I could never afford to, yeah, but – I'm honest!' She feels so insecure and restless in her bleak marriage and vulnerable financial position that she says: 'I feel all the time like a cat on a hot tin roof.' She is 'consumed with envy and eaten up with longing'. She is furious with Brick who has the 'charm of the defeated'. Brick himself is so 'detached' that his main concern is to wait for the ominous 'click' that signals he has enough alcohol: 'The click I get in my head when I've had enough of this stuff to make me peaceful.' He and Maggie do not live together: 'We occupy the same cage.' Their marriage is destroyed by the memory of the relationship with Skipper a 'beautiful ideal thing' in Brick's mind, which she despoils for him by 'naming it dirty'.

After the outburst between Big Daddy and Big Mama, he wonders if it might be true that she loved him after all: '*Wouldn't it be funny if that was true* . . . ' An example of the parlous state of relations within the family occurs in Act Three when Big Mama embraces Brick, ignoring Gooper, saying: 'you know we just got to love each other . . .' as Gooper stands behind her '*tense with sibling envy*'.

Other approaches to the play could concentrate on any one of the themes discussed in the 'Commentary' section, on structure, on the tragic or comic elements in the play, (see 'The nature of the play', p. 29), or on character. All of these are covered in the relevant section, with accompanying relevant quotations.

Preparing and presenting an essay

It is probably fair to assume that most readers of *Cat on a Hot Tin Roof* who are working to acquire academic qualifications will at some time be asked to write at least one essay of about fifteen hundred words. A week or a fortnight will be given for the completion of the task and direct access to the principal text and to secondary authorities will not be prohibited. What preparation does such an essay require? How is it to be written? What should it contain?

We may usefully begin by distinguishing between general preparedness and special preparations. Having read the play carefully several times, having seen it staged, or having taken part in it (as outlined above) will result in most students being generally prepared to write an essay. However, an essay question will invite consideration of specific aspects of the play that may have escaped the attention of even a well-prepared student. In these circumstances it is best to read the play once again, with the question firmly in mind, carefully noting incidents and speeches and turns of phrase that will be relevant to an answer.

Many students have great difficulty in distinguishing what is relevant from what is not, and yet, in the vast majority of cases, all that is needed in making the distinction is a little common sense. The clue to what is relevant is usually contained in the question itself. For example: a question like 'Tennessee Williams wrote: "I don't want to talk to people, about the surface aspects of their lives . . ." How does *Cat on a Hot Tin Roof* explore the deeper aspects of personality and social situations?' does not invite you to write about background or setting or context of the play; nor does it ask you to analyse its language. The clues here are the quotation from Williams himself, and the direction or 'steer' the examiner has given you. The quotation indicates that Williams, as a writer, regarded himself as being intent on getting at the hidden truth behind the surface; and the steer asks you to look at personalities and the situations with which they find themselves having to cope. You are here being directed to the *core* of the play: that network of key issues and concerns that form the tissue of human difficulty that the playwright wishes to probe into. See the specimen answers in this section for a model attempt at this question.

Different people will answer the same question in different ways and there are often legitimate differences of opinion over what a good answer should contain. There is, however, broad agreement among markers over what an essay should *not* contain. Bear the following points in mind:

(a) Very few questions (and no good ones) require a student simply to tell again in his own words the plot of a play. Use plot summary sparingly and only when the question cannot be answered without such a summary.

(b) Quotations from primary material (from the text of Williams's play and from any other play with which you are comparing it) should usually be brief and ought only to be included when they have a definite part in forwarding the argument of your essay. Decorative quotations, introduced merely to indicate your knowledge of the text, should be avoided.

(c) When deciding whether or not to include quotations from secondary material (from books or articles about Williams), the most stringent tests of relevance should be applied.

(d) When you introduce your chosen quotation avoid hackneyed formulas, e.g.: 'It is important to remember that Tennessee Williams is amongst the greatest modern American dramatists.' Secondary authorities frequently set a bad example themselves in this respect.

(e) Do not quote what you do not understand, and never fall into the trap of supposing that it must be worth quoting because you do not understand it. Not all academic authors write clearly or well: there is no advantage to be gained from solemnly introducing into your essay material which will disfigure it; its presence there will call your own good judgement into question.

(f) Direct use of secondary material (quotation) must always be acknowledged directly. In a classroom essay the author's name, the title of the book, and a page reference should follow the quotation in parentheses. Failure to acknowledge quotations, and, worse still, failure to indicate that they are quotations, is a serious matter which often leads to an essay being rejected in its entirety. Indirect use of secondary material should also be acknowledged – by means of a list of 'Books Used' or 'Bibliography' at the end of your essay. Where the details or direction of an argument, though not the wording itself, are borrowed from another author, specific acknowledgement of the borrowing is proper and in more advanced essay work it is essential. In short, acknowledge indebtedness openly, but do not confuse the nervous accumulation of secondary authorities with sound scholarship.

Specimen questions

(1) 'Communication is – awful hard between people . . .' Consider the relevance of Brick's observation to the structure and or characterisation of *Cat on a Hot Tin Roof.*
(2) Tennessee Williams wrote: 'I don't want to talk to people only about the surface aspects of their lives . . .' How does *Cat on a Hot Tin Roof* explore the deeper aspects of personality and social situations?
(3) Maggie describes Brick as having 'the charm of the defeated'. Consider the theme of failure in *Cat on a Hot Tin Roof.*
(4) Discuss lies and lying in *Cat on a Hot Tin Roof.*
(5) Explore the ways in which the past is made use of in *Cat on a Hot Tin Roof.*
(6) Tennessee Williams described his aim in *Cat on a Hot Tin Roof* as 'trying to catch the true quality of experience in a group of people'. Discuss.

Specimen answers

(2) Tennessee Williams wrote: 'I don't want to talk to people only about the surface aspects of their lives . . .' How does *Cat on a Hot Tin Roof* explore the deeper aspects of personality and social situations?

As a dramatist Tennessee Williams was concerned to find a way of putting on stage what he describes, in a long stage direction in Act Two of *Cat on a Hot Tin Roof*, as 'the true quality of experience in a group of people', the 'interplay of live human beings in the thundercloud of a common crisis'. He wanted, in other words, to get to the heart of human interaction, which means that he saw the stage as a platform in which he could present characters in particular situations coming to the realisation that the 'surface aspects' of their lives may have very little relationship with what is going on underneath. The stage, the theatre, is a place for showing the true substance of things, what Williams called the 'discretion of social conversation'. The theatre, as the Greek origin of the word reveals, is a place for seeing things, and what you see in *Cat on a Hot Tin Roof* is human personality in a group of individuals, with the lid taken off. Williams also creates a set of human situations in which his characters are put under pressure, and this pressure forces them to confront hidden truths about themselves and others.

On the face of it the social situation which Big Daddy's family are in is a privileged one. Through effort and determination the old man has created a dynasty for his offspring, comprising a fine old Southern Plantation house, servants and a retinue of followers: the Reverend Tooker and Doc Baugh each defer to the monied landowner. His estate is extensive, ('28,000 acres of the richest land this side of the Valley Nile'), and he has reached a position of social eminence which allows free range to his personality. It looks as if he has achieved all a man could, and he is now in a position to exercise the freedom from restraint wealth and power can bring. However, as he quickly realises, he is a dying man, with the 'foxteeth' of cancer in his gut. But it is not just in this respect that his social situation is not what it seems. The entire network of family relations that surround him is in a state of turmoil and Williams's play concentrates on revealing the 'common crisis' shared by all. The fact that he observes the classical unities of space and time, in that the action on stage takes place in one setting and unfolds in the time the events themselves would occupy in actuality, increases the sense the play conveys of depth and intensity, of getting beneath the surface to the terrible truths these lives keep hidden.

Williams carefully shapes his play so that the main characters reveal their true natures in situations of conflict, confrontation, or crisis. Each of the three Acts concentrates on specific groupings of characters and inter-actions or collisions between them. Act One deals with the 'quality of experience' in marriages, focusing primarily on Brick and Maggie's, but contrasting it with that between Gooper and Mae and Big Daddy and Big Mama. The Brick–Maggie marriage is not only childless, it is also deeply unstable, and relies upon Maggie observing what Brick calls the 'laws of silence'; that she, in other words, will not attempt to discuss the reasons for Brick's unhappiness and his alcoholism. Up till now she has kept his 'law' (he is like his father in insisting on laws and edicts), but Big Daddy's terminal illness has awakened her to the precariousness of their situation: 'it takes money to take care of a drinker', and unless she moves now, and does something to awaken Brick from his alcoholic stupor, they will be left with nothing. The technique she uses to achieve this is to confront her husband with the reason for his emotional inertia, his drinking, and his lack of interest in her. This, she says, is the love that Skipper, his old college-friend and team-mate, had for Brick. Brick protests that what was between them was friendship, but Maggie, to her husband's horror and fury, tells him that one drunken night while Brick was laid up with an injury, she confronted Skipper with her certainty that both she and he were in love with her husband. Afterwards, in a pathetic attempt to prove her wrong, he tried to have sex with her. From then on, Skipper took to the bottle and ruined himself, before eventually dying. What she did, she says, was to say something about human personality that their social situations and conventions could not tolerate. Her searing analysis of this emotional triangle concludes with her assertion that death (Skipper's death) was the only outcome allowable for the men's feelings for each other. Brick protests that she is naming his friendship with Skipper 'dirty', while she responds that the only way to keep it pure was to preserve it in the 'icebox' of death. In effect she is saying to Brick that their marriage is based upon a killing: each of them, in their different ways, helped to kill Skipper. This troubled marriage, and the difficult human and personal misery hidden within it, form the emotional centre of the play. It is contrasted with Gooper and Mae's, an avid affair of convenience, opportunity, and advancement.

It is also contrasted with that between Big Daddy and Big Mama, which is based as much on her capacity for deluding herself that her rancorous man has loved her, as it is on his indifference. In Act Two Big Daddy destroys the birthday party his wife has arranged for him by accusing her of waiting for him to die so she can take over; 'sashaying your fat old body around the place I made' is how he describes what she has been doing for the past three years. His hatred and physical loathing of her now emerge in all ferocity in the incongruous setting of a birthday party called to celebrate Big Daddy's age and dignity, but also his (false) release from the threat of death. Big Mama now realises that the man she loved, despite his hardness and brutality, never believed that she felt anything for him. She has been nurturing the tragic illusion that she was truly appreciated in spite of her husband's cold behaviour. Now she has to face the fact that beneath his cold contempt for her there lies no love or tenderness.

Act Two then moves to its crisis. After the emotional exchange between Big Daddy and Big Mama, Brick and his father engage in a long dialogue (with a number of intrusions) in which the deeply unstable relationship between father and son is laid bare. Brick is his father's favourite, Big Daddy has as much contempt for Gooper, Mae and their five children as he has for his wife. But Brick he admires and feels close to. We learn that they have had conversations in the past but they have failed to communicate ('communication is – awful hard between people', Brick says), real contact between their two personalities has never 'materialised' (again the word Brick uses). But tonight is going to be different. Big Daddy begins by trying to get Brick to admit why he drinks too heavily, as it dawns on him, for the first time, that his son is an alcoholic. Pressed,

Brick claims that he is disgusted with the 'mendacity' of the world, the lies that keep society lubricated but which betray personal truth. Big Daddy is hugely impatient with what he regards as an inadequate reply. To his mind the world is full of mendacity and people have to learn to live with it. He probes further beneath the surface, getting his son to admit that their relationship is founded on a respect for the true human personality of each of them, and then confronting him with a bold statement: 'you started drinkin' when your friend Skipper died'. This brings the audience back to the emotional revelation of Act One, when Maggie brought Brick face to face with what he cannot admit to in his feelings about his dead friend.

Big Daddy's bombshell detonates through Brick's drink-sodden personality and provokes him into another bout of wild defensiveness. To his amazement he finds that his father is perfectly ready to accept homosexuality (Big Daddy says he has grown 'tolerance') but he protests that friendship between men does not necessarily mean that they are 'fairies' or that they perform 'sodomy'. Big Daddy, however, presses on and asks Brick why Skipper cracked up and why he has also. Now Brick puts up his last defensive action to protect himself from the truth his father is pushing him towards by telling the story of Maggie's betrayal of him with Skipper. He twists it by insisting that Maggie put it into his friend's mind that they were homosexuals and that Skipper tried to prove it wasn't true, and when he failed his humiliation broke him. Brick tries, in other words, to put the blame on Maggie. His father will not accept this story, insisting that something remains untold, and eventually Brick admits that there was a phone call in which his friend told him he loved him. He had hung up and, as Big Daddy points out, did not face the truth with his friend. This is the lie that has been festering away in his personality and destroying his social relations. In retaliation Brick tells his father the truth about *his* situation: that he is dying of cancer after all. Big Daddy's furious roars at the world conclude Act Two, in which he accuses everyone of lying all the time.

In Act Three Gooper and Mae show their hand. Behind their ostentatious displays of affection for Big Daddy and Big Mama lies a carefully constructed proposal to take over the estate on the old man's death, thereby reducing Brick and Maggie to dependants. And even though Big Mama protests towards the end that they all 'just got to love each other', she cuts Gooper out of her embrace. She is still trying to hold on to the ideal of love, with part of her mind, even though she knows how riddled the family is with hatred, self-hate, greed, anger, and corruption. The play concludes in a mood of forlorn love as Maggie plans for a future in which their love may revive.

Cat on a Hot Tin Roof exposes the betrayal, corruption, anger, self-delusion, and hatred which lie beneath the surface in a vivid portrayal of a southern plantation family in decline. It also explores the ways in which people lie to themselves to protect themselves from truths and realities which, if admitted, break up the comfortable self-image needed to survive in the 'discretion' of social conventions.

---

(5) Explore the ways in which the past is made use of in *Cat on a Hot Tin Roof*.

The past has a powerful grip on the characters and action of *Cat on a Hot Tin Roof*. All, to one degree or another, are engaged upon telling stories of their own lives, and Williams's skill as a dramatist is revealed in his being able to show these narratives contending with each other in the psychological turmoil and emotional entanglements of the action.

Because theatre combines action with speech, what characters have to say matters greatly, unlike, say, in dance-theatre, where diction is often dispensed with altogether. In the theatre characters do not only react to what has been said to them, they also often tell their histories, so their reaction to situations is explained more thoroughly and given a psychological and emotional context. Good drama, therefore, presents an audience with a changing human situation, as it happens, and also, at the same time, unfolds the past of the characters, thereby increasing interest and coherence. An incompetent playwright will stop the action to tell the audience why such a person is reacting in such a way (although there can be exceptions, as in the plays of Bertolt Brecht, where this is done deliberately and heightens the dramatic tension rather than lessening it). On the whole a good playwright will allow the past circumstances to emerge naturally in the immediate flow of the dialogue's current. This co-ordination between past and present is handled extremely well in *Cat on a Hot Tin Roof*.

On a broad scale, the past is very much alive in the setting and background of the play. It takes place in a bedsitting room of a plantation home in the Mississippi Delta and although it is set in the time at which it was first performed, the mid-1950s, nevertheless the world it evokes has remnants of Old Southern grandeur. The estate is massive, 28,000 acres; the house is huge; there are servants and many field-hands; the whole scenario is a survival of a long-outmoded form of life belonging more to the 'Old South' of the late nineteenth century than to the modern world. It is a mode of life that is in decline, as the various tensions and breakdowns revealed in the action make clear; nevertheless some of the play's pathos resides in Big Mama's attempts to hold on to a façade of decency and love in a world which is driven by hatred and greed.

Big Daddy himself, the old plantation patriarch, turns out to have once been a hobo and a bum, travelling around the country, taking his chances in the poverty-stricken South of the early twentieth century, when the gulf between rich and poor was immense. He managed to cross that gulf by securing the interest and support of old Straw and Ochello, the original owners of the plantation, homosexuals who took the young man under their wing. Their experiences gave Big Daddy a practised tolerance in the world, making him virtually unshockable, and alert to lies, self-indulgence, and false emotion. It gave him a curious mix of tolerance and tough-mindedness, all of which emerges in the confrontation that forms the centre-piece of the play, the long dialogue between him and his son in Act Two. This dialogue is also of interest because it shows two different kinds of past, and attitudes thereto, in collision.

Big Daddy's colourful past emerges as he presses Brick to face up to why he is an alcoholic. When Brick declares that he is sick of the 'mendacity' of the world, where everyone lies through cowardice, indifference or deceit, Big Daddy refuses to take this seriously, maintaining that his own experience has taught him that mendacity is necessary. He has had to pretend to love his wife, his son Gooper, and his daughter-in-law Mae, with their five 'screechers'. And when he probes further, getting Brick to open up the homosexual nature of his friendship with Skipper, his dead ex-team-mate, the older man displays a sophisticated and worldly-wise imperturbability about the strangeness of the world: 'I seen all things and understood a lot of them, till 1910.' Jack Straw and Peter Ochello – two figures who feature largely in this play although they are dead – took Big Daddy in and got him to manage the estate. They were homosexuals, and when Straw died the other stopped eating and died too. This reminiscence is done in the heat of Big Daddy's probing analysis of his son's drinking problem, so it becomes charged with significance and is dramatically relevant to the unfolding psychological action. The past fuels and enriches and makes more complex and dangerous the evolving moment.

This danger is exemplified immediately in Brick's terror-stricken reaction: he accuses his father of thinking that he and Skipper 'did sodomy'. Shouting through his father's commands to 'hold on a minute', Brick excitedly protests against his father's suggestion (as Brick sees it) that he and his friend, were, to use his words, 'ducking sissies', 'queers'. The strength of the son's protest is such as to indicate very clearly to the audience that the father has touched the truth; hence Brick's defensiveness. The older man can live with the past, and the present – he admits he hates his wife, and has always hated her – but Brick cannot face his own personal history, nor the present. The past he converts into various histories, the present he blurs with drink, waiting for the 'click', which shuts off the brain, just in case the truth may surface. Brick has three versions of his tangled relationship with Skipper: the one he gives to Maggie, which is that it was a pure friendship; the next is that which he offers his father, that it was a pure friendship until Maggie put the dirty thought into Skipper's head that they were homosexuals, a thought that destroyed his friend; and the third is the last one, dragged out of him by his father's questioning, that Skipper confessed to Brick that he loved him during a drunken conversation.

Big Mama, Maggie, and Mae also, in their different ways, are struggling with the meaning and burden of the past. Big Mama has cultivated a notion of love, which is blasted by the furious declaration of truth her husband makes when he thinks he has recovered. In spite of this blow to her own understanding of her past and her personality in the present, she still tries to cling to a notion of love in Act Three, in spite of the evidence of emotional breakdown and turmoil all around. Maggie's past was insecure, and made her familiar with poverty, so that now she is resolved to hold on to as much of the estate as she can. Furthermore, she was crucially involved in a triangular relationship with Brick and Skipper, and has been a scapegoat for Brick's guilt about his friend for years, thus providing him with an emotional equivalent to the chemical soft option of alcohol. Mae is like Maggie in one respect: she too has a past, even shadier than Maggie's, making her just as determined to secure the estate for her husband.

Cat on a Hot Tin Roof shows us a group of characters in the grip of the past, compelled, for various reasons, to face up to its implications in the present.

---

(6) Tennessee Williams described his aim in *Cat on a Hot Tin Roof* as 'trying to catch the quality of experience in a group of people'. Discuss.

Tennessee Williams makes this comment in the middle of a lengthy stage direction in Act Two, at a crucial emotional turning point in the play, when Big Daddy and Brick come to the climax of the conversation that forms the core of the dramatic action. Although there are only two people involved in this exchange, the sensual and venal father and his hopelessly 'detached' and alcoholic son, nevertheless this exchange lays bare the unhappiness, instability, and loneliness that troubles the Pollitt family.

We learn that this conversation is the culmination of many such encounters between the wilful old man and his ruined son, except that previously they have gone 'round in circles'. Brick himself says to his father, hesitating as he does so, 'Communication is – awful hard between people an' – somehow between you and me, it just don't – '. Here the dashes are meant to be theatrical pauses, full of tension, to make the audience expectant and uneasy. Although communication is difficult in this play, where people lie to each other and to themselves (Doc Baugh lies to Big Daddy and Big Mama; Brick lies to himself about Skipper), nevertheless the action of Act Two brings these problems to a head. The detachment Brick has cultivated will be broken, and Big Daddy's blustering renewal of confidence will be shown to be a lie. Father and son confront each other with unpalatable truths – Brick's probable homosexuality and Big Daddy's imminent death – releasing a dynamic energy at the end of Act Two. The family can now no longer be the same. Big Mama will discover in Act Three that the harsh and brutal man she has loved will die; she will realise that her son, Gooper, only thinks of his own advantage; and she will discover the strength to resist Gooper's plan to take over the estate, despite her hysteria and shock.

The complicated sets of relations between the various members of this family are brought home to us following the exchange between father and son. We are surprised that it is Big Daddy who is tolerant of homosexuality while his son cannot accept the possibility that he may have such inclinations. It is the son who is, for all his 'charm' and detachment, narrow and repressed; while the dying man, for all his brutality, has tenderness and understanding.

The different agendas different people have (Williams as a dramatist was always eager to register the different ways in which people see the world) also become clear in this play, helping to convey the 'quality of experience in a group of people'. Maggie and Mae are intent, in their different ways, on getting hold of as much as they can of Big Daddy's wealth, but Maggie is desperate, Mae merely calculating. Brick and Gooper are entirely different sons, but Brick, like Maggie, has more emotional honesty, even though he lacks the courage to face the full facts of his friendship with Skipper. Big Mama longs for love; Big Daddy has a hankering, still, for sex. He also seems to have been oblivious to the fact that he has been loved for many years.

This family is in a critical condition. They attack each other, are intolerant, unforgiving and selfish, yet what emerges is a 'quality of human experience' which is all the more convincing because while the play conveys the harshness of human nature, it also shows us people who are lonely, confused, and sad.

A note on examinations

The essential point to be made about examinations, at whatever level you encounter them, is that they are best regarded as the natural conclusion to a course of study. Questions on *Cat on a Hot Tin Roof* are designed to test the quality of your understanding of the play, developed over a long period of time. They are not designed to allow you to display how much of the text you have managed to commit to memory in the preceding few days.

Preparing for an examination is not a special sort of activity, undertaken after you have finished reading Williams's play and no longer have to think about it. Preparation, moreover, is not an activity that you should confine to the last few weeks or days of your academic term. Above all, those frenzied last-minute revision stints which so many students inflict upon themselves are best avoided. All save the most aggressively competitive students are likely to be harmed by them, and they frequently destroy any hope of a student's ever again enjoying the work upon which he or she is being examined. In English studies the mere swot is at a disadvantage. There are no formulas to be learned, or lists of irregular verbs to be mastered, and committing to memory a few striking scenes or snatches of dialogue, though sometimes a useful exercise, is not sufficient to guarantee success in an examination.

This last point needs to be looked at more carefully since many students think that an examination is designed to test their knowledge of an author, and think in addition that 'knowing an author' equals being able to recite the words that he has written. An examination, however, is properly designed to test the quality of your understanding of an author's work, and merely reciting his words, however accurately, will not satisfy the requirements of such a test. What matters is whether the words which you cite support and illustrate and help to advance your argument. If they do not do so they are irrelevant, and ought not to be included. It is within the examination room itself that you will need to recollect those parts of Williams's play that are relevant to your answer: the danger in learning lists of quotations by heart a few days before the examination is that you will include them in your answer merely because you know them, without regard to their relevance.

Many students, who in the ordinary course of events have no difficulty in thinking clearly on quite complex matters, are nevertheless worried when they are told that they will have to think during an examination. This worry frequently leads them into the grip of one of the unhappiest of all malpractices: question-spotting. Reading past examination papers in order to see what sort of questions are likely to be set is a wise use of your time, but do not forget that you are sitting this year's examination, not last year's. Your examiners have the right to set questions which they think proper, and a duty to avoid setting questions which simply reproduce those of former years. Examinations test your responsiveness to the question that is in front of you; your ability to answer last year's question will impress no one. Never prepare answers in advance.

What lies behind question-spotting and answering in advance is the fear which many students have that under examination pressure their minds will go blank as soon as they put pen to paper. For most students, however, there is no real danger that this will happen, provided that preparation has been thorough, relaxed, and of the right kind. Such preparation takes time and cannot be hurried but since it is indistinguishable from a serious and interested study of your text, whether in the library or in the theatre, it is pleasurable and rewarding in itself, quite apart from the benefits which it confers in the examination room.

Part 5

Suggestions for further reading

The text

WILLIAMS, TENNESSEE: *Cat on a Hot Tin Roof and Other Plays*, Penguin, Harmondsworth, 1976.

Memoirs and interviews

WILLIAMS, TENNESSEE: *Memoirs*, W. H. Allen, London, 1976.
VIDAL, GORE: 'Selected Memories . . .' in *Matters of Fact and Fiction*, Vintage, New York, 1978.

Biographies

SPOTO, DONALD: *The Kindness of Strangers: The Life of Tennessee Williams*, The Bodley Head, London, 1985.

Critical works

LEAVITT, R. (ED.): *The World of Tennessee Williams*, G. P. Putnam's Sons, New York, 1978.
LOUDRE, F. H.: *Tennessee Williams*, Frederick Ungar, New York, 1979.

The author of these notes

Robert Welch is Professor of English at the University of Ulster, Coleraine; before that he taught at Leeds, Ife in Nigeria, and Cork. His critical books include *Irish Poetry from Moore to Yeats* (1980), *Changing States: Transformations in Modern Irish Writing* (1993), and he has edited *W. B. Yeats: Writings on Irish Folklore, Legend, and Myth* (1993) as well as *The Oxford Companion to Irish Literature* (1996). *The Kilcolman Notebook* (1994) is a novel, and *Muskerry* (1992) poems.